FADING ADS OF

MILWAUKEE

ADAM LEVIN

THE
History
PRESS

Published by The History Press
Charleston, SC
www.historypress.com

All images photographed by the author.

First published 2020

Manufactured in the United States

ISBN 9781467141987

Library of Congress Control Number: 2019951854

"Everyone has their own path..this is mine."
—Adam Levin

CONTENTS

ACKNOWLEDGEMENTS

With my most sincere gratitude, I want to thank Michelle Lalicata for her tireless efforts and tremendous contributions toward the production of this book.

INTRODUCTION

Amid the burgeoning city expansion, revitalization and progress, one can catch a glimpse into a bygone era. Fading ads marked the once-flourishing businesses from decades prior. One will see these hidden gems among the high-rise buildings in downtown Milwaukee and nestled into surrounding neighborhoods such as Walker's Point, Brewer's Hill and the Third Ward. From drugstores and supper clubs to beer bottlers and tanneries, from bowling alleys to local watering holes, they are reminiscent of life in Milwaukee from the late 1800s to the 1960s.

Some were once vibrant, hand-painted murals etched into brick building façades. Others lit up the evening sky with neon—flashy and exuberant. They ranged from simple and restrained to complex and extravagant; all proudly displayed by the owner. These signs were not simply "advertisements" or geographic markers. They represented freedom, expression, creativity, entrepreneurship, opportunity and success. They were reflections of Milwaukee's diverse culture.

Conveniently situated on Lake Michigan, Milwaukee was a booming port city in the early 1900s and a beacon of hope for thousands of European immigrants. Neighborhoods were settled by various ethnic groups, dominated by the Poles, Germans and Italians, each distinct for its culture and language. Each neighborhood had its own flair, and the businesses and signs reflected the culture and needs of the community.

These signs have borne witness to the rise of modern capitalism and individualism. Some have weathered the storms of the Great Depression.

Many others survived to see the light again well into the postwar economic boom. Today, they are steadily disappearing to make way for a "new" time. Those that remain are faded, decayed and neglected—soon to be a distant memory. But they are forever preserved in these photos.

1

EAST SIDE

We start our journey into the history of Milwaukee through the faded murals and metal signs decorating the landscape of the East Side. It is bordered on the east and west by two bodies of water, Lake Michigan and the Milwaukee River, respectively, with boundaries extending north to the border of suburban Shorewood (Edgewood Boulevard) and as far south as East Juneau Avenue, adjacent to the Yankee Hill neighborhood. Many residents will reply with nondefinitive answers about where the official borders begin and end, but the majority will state that it is the "area near the lake nestled between the northern edge of downtown and the southern border of Shorewood." Within the East Side are several neighborhoods, such as Murray Hill, and the appropriately named "Lower" and "Upper" East Side. Some of the main arteries are North Avenue, Brady Street, Prospect Avenue and Oakland Avenue. The East Side is also home to the University of Wisconsin–Milwaukee campus. To pinpoint the exact location, locals will often refer to an area of interest as the "Brady Street area," "UW-M" or "North Avenue," for example.

Interestingly enough, each area has a collectively similar, yet different, vibe. As a whole, since the 1960s, the East Side has been referred to as "trendy" and as the "cultural hotspot" of Milwaukee. It also has been arguably the most metropolitan and diverse area of the city for decades. Here, all are represented: university students, young professionals, families and retirees. The socioeconomic demographic is predominantly middle to upper-middle class, but closer to Lake Michigan, mansion-like estates line the boulevard of what had been coined the "Gold Coast." While new condominiums and apartments have graced the landscape in recent years, the vast majority of housing dates to the period between the 1880s and 1930s.

The East Side was settled in the 1870s, primarily by Polish immigrants, followed by Italians. It is no surprise that the architecture is a mix of Queen Anne, Victorian, Italianate, Colonial Revival and Polish flats. An internet search on "Polish flat" reveals top results referencing Milwaukee. More Polish flats exist in Milwaukee than anywhere else in the United States. They help us reflect on a time when multigenerational families lived together and, particularly during the Great Depression, when families rented to "boarders" to ease financial burdens. As a result, an abundance of duplexes and multifamily housing remains today, making this a profitable playground for real estate investors.

AIR GLIDE

One of the most exuberant areas of the East Side is inarguably the Brady Street area. Located on the corner of Water and Brady Streets, the beautiful Air Glide advertisement remained relatively unblemished after spending decades in hiding. Construction crews must have been astonished to discover an inner wall, revealed during the demolition of the Comedy Café in November 2017.

Well preserved with minimal signs of fading, the sign is very legible: "Air Glide—Pate Gasoline Has No Equal! The block cutout obscures several words, but as the Pate slogan proclaimed, "Just a Fill—Feel the Difference!" At the bottom, "Motor Tune-Up" and "Brake Service" promote the additional services offered from what was at one time a full-service auto shop.

After extensive records research and informal conversations with local residents, I gleaned little about this service station from decades ago: who owned it, and when was it in operation? History leads us to draw several conclusions. Pate Oil Company was a Milwaukee-based petroleum distributor that was started by William R. Pate in 1933. Pate's gasoline, trademarked as "Air Glide" in 1947, claimed to reduce vehicle maintenance costs due to the higher octane levels with Pate Oil's Premium gasoline. Its performance claims were later proven to be true, as cars using Air Glide gasoline did indeed fare better, requiring fewer maintenance and repair servicing than cars using competitors' gasoline. Standard Oil, based in New Jersey, acquired Pate Oil in 1956 via stock exchange valued at nearly $5 million. Pate eventually became a part of Humble Oil, the operating company of Standard Oil, ultimately becoming part of the Enco brand.

According to a *Milwaukee Sentinel* article dated April 12, 1960, it was announced that the Enco name would start to replace the Air Glide name on the 211 gas stations throughout southeastern Wisconsin, with the rollout on May 8 of the same year. Over four hundred owners, dealers and gas attendants were informed of this decision by the vice-president of sales for Pate, James E. Dornoff, at a dinner meeting at the Wisconsin Club.

From this information, it is safe to say that this service station was serving the public throughout the 1950s and perhaps into the early 1960s at the very latest. Since the sign was never changed to reflect the rebranding from Air Glide to Enco, it is doubtful that it was open far beyond 1961. Once again, we are led to assume that it was close to this time that the service station closed. New owners, after removing the gas pumps, evidently walled

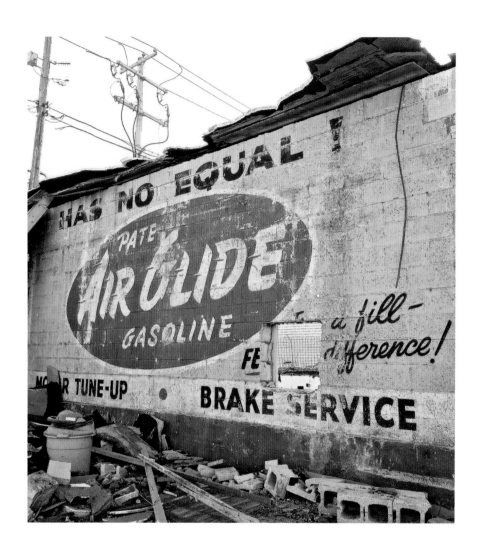

ABOVE This Air Glide/Pate Oil sign was buried behind a wall after demolition of the Comedy Café on Brady Street in late 2017.

off the area, creating an outer wall. The wall boasting this ad, as a result, was hidden on what was transformed to an inside wall.

Take a moment to reflect on what that this painted ad may have meant to the owner and the community. How did the rebranding and takeover of Pate Oil play a role in the untimely demise of this station? I can picture a once-flourishing business where loyal service attendants proudly represented Pate Oil, the hometown distributor. They would be dressed in neatly pressed uniforms embroidered with the Pate logo and sporting crisp hats, polished shoes and button-down shirts finished with a bowtie or necktie. It was an honor to serve their customers and community, whom they would delight with exemplary service. They would cheerfully chat with their customers about the value of their premium gasoline: "There is no equal! Just a fill! Feel the Difference!" proclaiming this as a guarantee. They were so confident in the high-quality gasoline they were selling that they knew the customer would return, securing a customer for life. With a genuine smile, they would fill customers' pumps while asking about their day and their family and perhaps sharing a joke or two.

Did the former owner of this station become soured with the takeover? Were these doors shut before the sale in 1957, or did it occur several years after? Did this owner attend the meeting in 1961 announcing the branding changes?

We do not know the answer to these questions. Everything at this point is pure speculation. It is the mystery behind this sign and many others like it. This is precisely what makes faded ads so intriguing.

Sadly, the wall with this treasure was demolished in January 2018, just two months after it was unearthed. As the land was prepared for the next establishment at 615 East Brady Street, the Up-Down arcade bar, I visited the construction grounds seven months later. A conversation with one of the construction workers revealed that "unplanned" work needed to be performed, as it was discovered that the ground was contaminated. In all likelihood, gasoline and other automotive fluids from this 1950s gas station were the primary contributors to the polluted soil.

Once the soil has been removed from the premises, this Pate Oil/Air Glide station, with no physical remnants remaining, will truly be a ghost from the past.

SCHLITZ

Tucked away in a residential area near Riverside Park just east of the Milwaukee River, a large mural faces the west and outlines the front half of a two-story apartment building. Although the red façade has been badly weathered over the years, the outlined advertisement is still clear: "Schlitz—The Drink That Made Milwaukee Famous." And indeed it did!

While it may seem odd to find a beer sign in a residential area, it is not so to the native Milwaukeean. It is simply part of the texture of the city. Neighborhood taverns were plentiful following Prohibition and are still prevalent today. Local watering holes were often bustling with patrons as early as seven in the morning, accommodating the overnight manufacturing and warehouse shift worker. Weekday late-afternoon hours were also bustling with dayshift laborers just ending their workday and looking for a few beers and, perhaps, a game of cards with their buddies before retiring home to their family for the evening.

The history of Schlitz brewery stretches back to its inception in 1849, when it was founded by August Krug, who introduced his brewing method and formula from his native Germany. Shortly after Krug Brewery launched, Krug hired another German immigrant, Joseph Schlitz, as his bookkeeper. Sadly, Krug's untimely death in 1856 led to the dissolution of the Krug Brewery. Knowing the business well, Schlitz took the reins as owner and assumed full management of the brewery. He subsequently changed the name to Joseph Schlitz Brewing Company after marrying Krug's widow. Krug's nephew, August Uihlein, also started working for the brewery and would eventually play an integral role in its executive leadership. By 1902, Schlitz had become the largest brewery in the United States. After Prohibition ended in 1934, Schlitz not only quickly regained the title as the leading U.S. brewer but also laid claim to being the best-selling brewery globally.

Schlitz Brewery enjoyed outstanding success and, during the height of production, it employed three thousand Milwaukeeans in the downtown factory and business offices.

OPPOSITE Schlitz Brewing sign on the Lower East Side, across the street from the Urban Ecology Center. The sign must have been retouched during Prohibition, as the company's slogan was "The beer that made Milwaukee famous."

However, the tides began to shift for the brewery in the 1950s. In 1953, thousands of workers went on a seventy-six-day strike, crippling production and ultimately resulting in Schlitz relinquishing its longtime number-one status to St. Louis–based brewery Anheuser-Busch. The battle for the top rank among breweries continued between these two giants into the mid-1970s.

They say hindsight is 20/20, and one can only speculate how the landscape of U.S. breweries might look today had a different course of action been taken.

In 1967, Robert Uihlein, grandson of August, made the costly and ultimately disastrous decision to alter the brewing process and formula that had been introduced by Krug, with the goals of reducing production costs while simultaneously increasing output. Essentially, the formula reduced the amount of malted barley and replaced it with corn syrup. Silica gel was added to the formula, and a cheaper grade of extracts replaced the high-quality ingredients that had been used for over a century. The traditional fermentation method was altered and replaced with a quicker, high-temperature fermentation process. The end result was a beer that lost the flavor to which millions had grown accustomed and enjoyed while also decreasing the shelf life. Schlitz's problems were exacerbated by stricter regulations set forth by the U.S. Food and Drug Administration for food and beverage labeling. Since Uihlein did not want consumers to see the ingredient "silica gel" listed on beer cans, a new agent, "Chill-Garde," was implemented into the process. This decision proved to be even more destructive to the brewery. This additive reacted horribly with the foam stabilizer, resulting in the recall of ten million bottles of beer across the world in 1975. Consequently, the company suffered a $1.4 million loss. An equally disastrous marketing campaign in 1977 and a worker strike in 1981 were more than this brewing giant could handle. Once the pride of Milwaukee, Schlitz went down in flames. It was a disastrous ending for this onetime brewing giant, which closed its doors in 1982, upon acquisition by Stroh Brewery of Detroit.

The Uihlein family and Schlitz name still maintain a tremendous presence in Milwaukee, despite the demise of the brewery. Philanthropic efforts and generosity abound. The Uihlein family has donated millions to the Milwaukee community over the years in support of art, nature and family entertainment. Milwaukee's Performing Arts Center bears the family name in the grand Uihlein Hall. The Schlitz Audubon Nature Center, located in Fox Point on the shores of Lake Michigan, provides education and supports conservation efforts, as well as being a gorgeous location for weddings and private events. Millions of dollars have been donated over the years to the Milwaukee County Zoo, the Milwaukee Public Museum and the Milwaukee Polo Club. The Uihlein and Schlitz families were once proud sponsors of the now-defunct Circus World Museum Fourth of July parade held in downtown Milwaukee.

This sign reminds us of Schlitz in its heyday: the global leader in brewing proudly produced in Milwaukee. The symbol in the middle, now badly faded, was of the globe wrapped with the Schlitz sash, representing the company's global dominance. Slowly, the history, like the sign, is fading away.

USED CARS

Nearly illegible, the former home of East Side Chevrolet on Prospect and North Avenues boasts "Used Cars." The remainder of the message has completely worn away following decades of exposure to the elements. On closer examination, you can faintly make out the word "Motor" above "Used Cars." While far from an exciting message or design, I find this sign to be quite intriguing. Unlike other advertisements that were painted directly onto the brick façade, this sign was etched into a pure white concrete slab, several inches thick, built directly into the wall. It is almost as if the concrete sidewalk below was simply extended upward onto the wall, where the advertisement was painted decades ago. Also of note: this sign is at ground level, which was unusual, as most were erected several stories above to capture more viewers from afar. Physically jutting into the sidewalk, the concrete extends approximately five feet high and sits adjacent to a one-car service garage that is still in use today.

The building was erected in 1912, while the first documented car dealer was an Oldsmobile dealer by the name of Lake Park Motors Inc. Subsequent owners were Bob Black in the 1950s, East Side Chevrolet in the 1960s and, finally, Bud Donahue Chevrolet. Although it is unclear when this sign was built, it was a Lake Park Motors advertisement in a 1937 *Milwaukee Journal* advertisement that proclaimed, "Every used car we sell must RUN AND LOOK LIKE NEW." Does this directly reference the "Used Cars" etched in stone? Due to the significant decay, we can safely conclude that the sign is at least sixty years old. Perhaps the top line, now too faded to read, did indeed at one time read "Lake Park," while the second line read "Motors."

At the time of this writing, no effort has been made to remove either the sign or the concrete slab in which it is engraved. Eventually, the writing will disappear, leaving future generations to pause and reflect on what this once was.

OPPOSITE East Side Chevrolet. Before Prospect Mall was converted in 1976, the building was home to numerous car dealers.

SIEGEL'S

Haphazardly strewn boxes and trash lie among a fading sign reading simply "Siegel Entrance." The building was once home to Siegel's Liquor, a family-run establishment, and this sign graced what was formerly an exterior wall. Residing in a perfect location, nestled on the perimeter of the University of Wisconsin–Milwaukee campus and on the high-trafficked street of Oakland Avenue, Siegel's enjoyed a run of fifty-five years. Having opened in 1945, Siegel's Liquor saw business flourish, eventually prompting the need for more space. As part of the expansion, this particular section of the former parking lot was converted into an enclosed storage area. The "Siegel Entrance" was then closed off entirely from public view.

Loyal patrons were greeted with a smile—and a pretzel stick. Reportedly, it was common practice to close out the sale with the customer's choice of a pretzel rod or beef stick selected from the large jar sitting on the counter. Tremendous changes occurred year after year, from Blatz and Pabst midcentury to the advent of wine coolers in the 1980s and the surge of craft breweries in the mid-1990s. Despite many shifts and trends in American alcohol preferences, one thing remained constant: demand for alcohol.

Although the family continues to operate one location in Bay View, Jim Siegel retired and sold this location in 2000 to Otto's Wine and Spirits.

The Siegel's Liquor sign is not visible unless you have access to the back room. It was visible to the public before the addition over the parking lot.

SCHLITZ AND BLATZ AT AXEL'S INN

While this is not a painted mural, this gem still has a story to share. A dual-faced lighted Schlitz sign, visible from both the north and south, is perched on the second story of this 1903 red-brick building at 2860 North Oakland Avenue near the UW-M campus. The sign, at least sixty years old, is badly weathered and shows obvious indications of pervasive rust. Upon a closer look, it appears that at one time there may have been lights illuminating "Schlitz," based on the metal-pegged structures that constitute distinct points in each letter. The sign sits above Axel's Inn and is nestled between two residential windows.

Quietly gazing on the passersby below and beyond, the sign stands roughly two stories above street level and faces the east toward Lake Michigan and the sprawling UW campus. How many decades of college students has it observed walking through the doors below? Proclaiming "Schlitz on Draught," it silently beckons for all who desire a thirst for flavor and riveting, engaging conversation to enter the doors below. Axel's Inn, whose original owner was the driver for a member of the Uihlein family, has been tapping beer and pouring liquor shots since the late 1930s, shortly after the Great Depression. Many a student has imbibed at Axel's; there are even multiple accounts of UW professors holding their "office" hours at the far end of the bar. An unpretentious and no-frills "dive" bar, it has not changed much through the decades. The interior is dark, dated and tired. But that is exactly what makes Axel's so appealing. One always knows what to expect on entering. Somewhat bucking the latest trends in brewing and craft cocktails, Axel's, in all its simplicity, remains uniquely its own. Likewise, even though Schlitz is no longer served on tap, the sign remains as it always has: in its original form, withstanding the test of time.

Another brewing giant is proudly plastered on the red façade of 2867 North Oakland, on the second story in the rear of the building. It is white, faded to gray and overlaid—creating much of the background for the ad. Located on the same building that Axel's Inn calls home, this sign is obscured by trees when in bloom. Even though the first two letters are nearly illegible, one can still faintly read the iconic Blatz script with "Beer" painted in block font underneath, sealed with a six-pointed star. The first meaning that comes to many on seeing the star is that it must be the Star of David. Quite the contrary. Historically, in brewing, this is actually a symbol of alchemy and purity. Those brewers who associated the star with their brand proclaimed

that their brew consisted of all-natural ingredients and strictly adhered to sound brewing methods. In fact, the six points indicate the most prominent and important ingredients attributing to beer quality, flavor and consistency: water, hops, grain, malt, yeast and the brewer himself.

Blatz Brewing Company formed during the same period as other brewing giants in Milwaukee, such as Schlitz, Pabst and Miller. In 1852, Valentin Blatz merged his own brewery with City Brewery, formerly owned by Johann Braun, who had passed earlier that same year. Although not officially incorporated until 1889, the Valentin Blatz Brewing Company came out of the gates fast and furious. In 1875, Blatz was the first Milwaukee brewery to have the capability to bottle and ship nationwide. It was also ranked as Milwaukee's third-largest brewery in the early 1900s.

Sadly, Blatz brewery experienced a slow yet steady decline in the ensuing decades. Unable to keep pace with the other brewing leaders, Blatz was purchased by Pabst Brewing Company in 1958. However, after the federal government claimed that the purchase violated section seven of the Clayton Act, the sale was reversed in 1959. Nevertheless, Blatz ceased all operations that same year and sold all of its assets to Pabst in 1960. It can be presumed that perhaps another family-run establishment at one time took residence in the units below and next to Axel's Inn, commissioning the painting of this ad either immediately before or after Prohibition. Unfortunately, the paint is weathering quickly. It is completely hidden from public view, as it can be seen only while standing on the second-floor landing of the building. No efforts appear to be in place to restore or preserve it.

OPPOSITE TOP "Schlitz on Draught" sign above Axel's dive bar is a classic, but the neon is gone. Many generations have frequented this bar and continue to do so.

OPPOSITE BOTTOM Blatz at Axel's and Oakland Gyros. I was very lucky to get permission to take this photo. I went to the second floor of the building, which is an apartment through the back door of the patio.

GLORIOSO'S

Unless you are a local, trying to guess what this sign represents requires multiple turns on *Wheel of Fortune*: "Can I buy a vowel and a half dozen consonants?"

Since 1946, Glorioso's has been a mainstay on Brady Street, just west of Humboldt Boulevard. It was in this postwar time that the lower East Side of Milwaukee, from Brady Street extending from the east at North Farwell Avenue and west to Van Buren, was shifting from a mixed Polish, German and Irish neighborhood to one with an increasing Italian presence. Beginning in the 1950s and throughout the next twenty-five to thirty years, this stretch of land that covers just a little over half a mile was dominated by Italian merchants. Savory aromas and street peddlers abounded, and the chattering of the Italian language, often sprinkled with the Sicilian dialect, was pervasive. This "new" Italian neighborhood was flourishing and provided not only a place for all in the community to congregate but also a welcome comfort for all Sicilian and Italian immigrants who missed the sights and smells of their homeland.

Glorioso Brothers was founded by three sons of Felice Glorioso, who had emigrated from Sicily. Joe, Eddie and Ted Glorioso opened their grocery store at this location and branched into several businesses in the following years. Through their wholesale business, they sold imported items such as olive oils, pasta, sauces and twenty-four-karat gold in both modern and traditional settings, along with religious medals. Their rich variety of imported cheese, sausages, salads and pastas were all prepared in the traditional ways from the homeland. The unmistakable draw into their store, however, was the alluring aroma.

The sign, simple and underwhelming in design, was reflective of exactly who the Glorioso brothers were: humble, kind and driven with a strong work ethic and love for their heritage. They were passionate about their work and the community they served, and they took seriously the need to provide for their families. They represented the American dream: turning a $1,000 loan and a wheel of parmesan into a grand success. Glorioso's is no longer at this location and the sign has since been removed, but the family moved the prosperous business across the street and expanded the store from one thousand square feet to ten thousand. The sign gently reminds us that, sometimes, the old needs to step down to make way for the new. Per their website, the Glorioso family proudly states, "Making New Traditions—One

Meal at a Time." And that is exactly what they have accomplished. While still remembering their earlier struggles and holding on to their beginnings, they continue to expand and explore new endeavors, all of which have allowed them to retain their tremendous base while simultaneously drawing customers from all over the city and beyond.

ABOVE Glorioso's. This building was vacant for nearly a decade on Brady Street. The store was remodeled by the family, and the old sign was exposed underneath.

PABST

This collection would not be complete without one of the most famous and prominent of all Milwaukee breweries. Pabst Brewery was established in 1844 by the Jacob Best family, descendants of the Rhineland region of Germany. Frequently battling for the top spot with crosstown rival Schlitz, Pabst, initially known as the Philip Best Brewery, was the largest beer producer from 1874 until the early 1900s. In 1889, the brewery officially changed its name to Pabst Brewery, when Captain Frederick Pabst, son-in-law of Jacob Best, assumed ownership. Pabst seized every opportunity for expansion, including the acquisition of competing breweries and the expansion of real estate and operations to the East Coast. Pabst also realized profitable growth from the vast destruction of Chicago as a result of the 1871 fire. Several prestigious brewing medals were bestowed on Pabst, the first of which was a gold medal awarded in 1876. It was not until 1882 that Pabst began to market these achievements, celebrating with a hand-tied blue silk ribbon around the neck of each bottle of Best Select and Pabst Select. The slogan "Pabst Blue Ribbon Beer" took hold, and this practice continued until the early 1940s, with a brief interruption during Prohibition.

Pabst remained in the top five of all breweries until 1982 and employed tens of thousands of loyal Milwaukeeans for nearly a century. Milwaukeeans were proud of their beer, loyal to the brand and even more proud of their city. However, in 1986, the tone changed abruptly from one of pride to one of betrayal. Briefly following the announcement that more than eight hundred retirees would lose a significant portion of their pensions in the form of health and death benefits, the brewery ceased all operations at the Milwaukee plant in December of that year. Pabst was purchased by the S&P Company in 1985, many ways marking the "beginning of the end" for one of the kings of breweries. Ask a Milwaukee native their opinion of Pabst and expect a variety of answers: the younger generation has seen the revival of the label as a "hipster beer" post-2010 and will generally speak with enthusiasm about their "hometown brew." However, the baby boomer generation will probably respond differently. Many in this generation feel that Pabst turned its back on the city that had supported it for 150 years—pride has mutated to bitterness and contempt.

OPPOSITE Pabst at Zaffiros. Located on Farwell Avenue, we find a reminder of the strong presence Pabst once had on the southern exterior wall. A Milwaukee favorite since 1954.

This Pabst sign sits on the southern exterior wall of Zaffiro's Pizza, a local pizza favorite established during the Brady Street Italian expansion in 1954. The sign appears to be from that time frame as well. The sign is approximately three feet in width and five feet in length. Showing signs of rust and decay, the print is still clearly legible. However, the bright white and royal blue trim has faded into achromatic shades of gray. This sign represents the "good ol' days," when Pabst was in its prime and peaked in popularity nationwide. Eliciting a wide range of emotions, the sign encourages us to remember Pabst as it was when the sign was mounted onto the side of the building: the beer that everyone in Milwaukee cherished.

2

DOWNTOWN

Anything but homogenous, downtown Milwaukee comprises four distinct neighborhoods, each possessing a distinct and unique vibe and history.

The business district lies within East Town, which encompasses the eastern portion of downtown. Bordered by Lake Michigan to the east and the Milwaukee River to the west and tucked between Ogden Avenue and Clybourn Avenue to the north and south, respectively, East Town represents all that is modern and progressive. Trendy restaurants and nightclubs flourish here, and Cathedral Square hosts some of the city's most popular outdoor festivals, such as summer favorites Jazz in the Park and Bastille Days, and the Festival of Lights in December. Unfortunately, many of the historical buildings that existed here were razed between the 1960s and 1980s to make way for skyscrapers and modern architecture styles.

Leaving East Town and heading west on Wisconsin Avenue, one cannot deny the striking contrast that exists as one traverses one of the many bridges over the Milwaukee River. It is akin to a portal of sorts—moving from one city into another. While East Town boasts fresh attitudes and progress, maintaining a tiny shred of the past in the historical sites that have survived, West Town appears somewhat neglected and lacks the vibrancy of its neighbor. Officially bordered by Interstate 794 and the Marquette University campus, possessing a dominant "urban" feel, West Town is indeed considered a focal point in entertainment, particularly in sports: the Fiserv Forum and US Cellular Arena host major-, minor- and university-level sports teams. The skyline is dominated by historic architecture, which, assuming these buildings can be restored, will lend a fantastic benefit to West Town, which is undergoing a revitalization and redevelopment by the city.

Formerly the "Warehouse District" of Milwaukee, several words adequately describe the Third Ward: intimate, trendy, artsy, historic. Heavily settled by Irish and Italian immigrants in the early 1900s, the area is now heavily populated by a diverse group of young professionals and is one of the most highly sought-after places to live. Many of the original warehouses remain and have been conserved and repurposed into loft-style apartments and condominiums. The area is rich with character and flair, hosting dozens of eclectic and locally owned eateries, coffeehouses, boutiques and art galleries.

Rounding out downtown, the Menomonee Valley neighborhood is in a state of revival and is the least populated of all downtown neighborhoods. Formerly dominated by in the railroad industry and heavy manufacturing, the Menomonee Valley is home to several parks and such attractions as the Potawatomi Casino, the Harley-Davidson Museum and Miller Park.

NELSON BROTHERS

In big, bold, block print, this sign reads simply, "Nelson Brothers." There is no indication about what Nelson Brothers is and the line of business in which they operated. There was no need to do so. They were large enough for their name to speak volumes, as their stellar reputation and name recognition preceded them. This is located at approximately the twelfth story and beyond, above street level, as the sign itself is three stories high and encompasses the entire width of the building. The painted ad itself faces south, which likely has protected it from the winds off Lake Michigan to the east. The background looks to have been at one time blue but has since faded into a darker gray. "Free Parking" is broadcast above, possibly as a lure to those who had fled to the suburbs and avoided downtown due to the lack of parking and expanded availability of goods outside the city limits.

Nelson Brothers. If you grew up in Milwaukee during the 1970s, you know the jingle: "Nelson Brothers loves me! And they'll love you, too."

Quite honestly—and only native Milwaukeeans born prior to 1980 would understand this—the first memory that hits me when I see the Nelson Brothers sign is not visual, nor do I recollect any experiences shopping at this location. Instead, I hear a jingle. A repetitive, kitschy yet catchy television commercial jingle from the 1970s that went something like this: "Nelson Brothers loves me! And they'll love you, too!" Nelson Brothers sold everything needed to decorate and furnish your home, from furniture to wall hangings, from lighting to rugs. And they sold it all at warehouse prices. At one point, they had seven locations throughout the Milwaukee area, making them one of the most popular, if not the leader, in furniture sales from the 1940s through the 1990s.

Formerly the home of Waldheim Furniture, Nelson Brothers Furniture moved into this 1916 ten-story brick structure. It is situated directly on the Milwaukee River to the east with an official address of 728 North Plankinton Avenue beginning in 1946. They remained at this location until 1990, and the structure was converted into condominiums in 1997.

MILK AND CREAM

While just shy of one city block outside the downtown limits, for the purposes of this book, this fascinating gem will be included in the West Town neighborhood. At 419 West Vliet Street is a beautiful, yet sorely neglected, Empire-style Cream City brick warehouse standing approximately two and one-half stories tall. The brick exterior has been painted with a robin egg blue, creating a striking contrast with the maroon doors. Constructed in 1888 by rag and paper merchant William P. Froehlich, it was purposed as a paper warehouse. However, just one short year later, in 1889, the building was converted into a laundry servicer as Wood Steam Laundry. Over the next one hundred plus years, the building switched hands dozens of times, encompassing a wide variety of industries. Beginning in 1919, Wobst Shoe Company was the primary occupant, until 1931, when it was replaced by Smartstyl Shoe Factory, which enjoyed a very brief stay here. Over the next

Froehlich Building. Many buildings in downtown Milwaukee have come and gone, but this one stands its ground. This building dates to 1888.

decade, these walls were almost solely inhabited by independent poultry and agriculture merchants such as Krasno Quality Egg Company, Marvelous Vegetable Yeast Company and Keipper Cooping Company. In the 1940s, the building switched to the tool, die and machinery industries: Reisen Chemical, B. Holtz Broom Company, Crest Engineering and Treichel Herman Machinery Shop, to name a few companies.

The block-lettered sign above and adjacent to the main entrance reads "Milk and Cream," leading one to believe that, at some point, a creamery was among the compelling list of occupants. The top line of the ad reads "Milk and Cream" while the second line is heavily obscured. At best guess, it appears that this reads "Bought." However, records and evidence of a creamery are difficult to find. Studying the timeline of the building occupants—from steam laundry to shoes; from agriculture to machinery—the logical assumption is that a creamery must have been here in the 1930s. After extensive research, the evidence indicates that, nearly thirty years earlier, the Champeny Creamery Company produced butter, cream and milk under this roof. Records support the notion that Champeny may have been at this location for approximately one year before moving to nearby 516 Chestnut Street (name later changed to Juneau Avenue).

The Champeny family, with Wisconsin roots dating back to the mid-1800s, originally hailed from England. In the late 1800s, two brothers, Charles C. and T.W. Champeny, established a chain of creameries throughout Milwaukee and Waukesha Counties. The Champeny Creamery prided itself on "Fancy Butter" and fresh products, differentiating itself from the competition with a "higher quality product" that would not get consumers sick.

As I reflect on that time in history, images flood into my mind of trucks bringing in milk freshly obtained from the nearby dairy farms for processing into milk and cream products. Many homes in Milwaukee, much like those across the United States prior to 1960, were constructed with built-in milk chutes. Doors opened to both the exterior and interior of the home, and the milkman would daily deliver milk on his route through this chute while retrieving the empty glass bottles from the prior delivery. This practice declined and eventually ceased completely in the mid-1970s in favor of the availability of fresh milk in the grocery aisles and rising costs for home delivery. I remember the experience quite vividly as a child: retrieving the fresh milk from our chute and placing the empty bottles afterward. Never to be forgotten, a predominant memory from my childhood is that milk in the clear glass jars—how fresh, flavorsome and delectable it tasted.

JOHN ERNST

Meticulous, bold and proudly boasting the title "Milwaukee's Oldest Restaurant," John Ernst Café was one of the three longtime old-world German establishments in downtown Milwaukee—Mader's and Karl Ratszch's were the other two. At the time of this writing, only Mader's remains. Opened in 1878, John Ernst closed its doors in May 2001. Times change.

People change. Tastes change. While Milwaukee is heavily rooted in German traditions and history, the taste for the richness of traditional German fare declined significantly in the late 1980s and the 1990s. While a love affair with sausage, cheese and beer continued, patrons shifted toward healthier, lighter and other "globally refined" options. The heaviness of traditional German dishes, such as Wiener schnitzel, goulash and sauerbraten, was indulged on special occasions, but certainly not on a frequent basis.

The sign itself has that wood-grain background, characteristic of the hardwood flooring, wall paneling and bars built from rich oak and mahogany in the many restaurants of this time and that were a part of the fabric of John Ernst's café. White linens and dim lighting rounded out this ambiance, conveying warmth and *gemütlichkeit* to its guests. The Ernst name is surrounded by three coats of arms linked together. The middle appears to be a chalice, graced on each side with what appears to be knives or utensils. Since these don't seem to represent any German geographic region, we can conclude that they are directly linked to food and beverage served by this fine-dining establishment. The sign, which appears to have undergone a recent restoration, has been perfectly preserved and remains untouched.

ABOVE John Ernst Café served great food in a community atmosphere. This place was one of the big three German restaurants in Milwaukee.

SKELLY'S AND SHERKOW'S

I like to refer to this as the "sprawling wall of dying traditions": luncheons and formal wear. Located in the rear of 622 West Wisconsin Avenue facing a parking lot, the remnants of two popular establishments from decades ago remain today. Built in 1917 in Gregorian Revival style, this was the former home of Skelly's Restaurant and Sherkow's Formal Wear. Encompassing the entire right façade of the building and scaling at least five floors is this ad for Skelly's Restaurant. The first two lines, while smudged, still legibly read "Skelly's Restaurant." The middle section in red is badly faded, but one can still make out "Wisconsin Ave." The script in the next section proclaims that it is "Milwaukee's Favorite." "Breakfast—Luncheon—Dinners—4 Dining Rooms" constitute the remainder of the block print. In white script overlaid on a green background, we are told that "A Century of Fine Food and Home Made Pastries" have been served.

Not much is known about when Skelly's opened its doors, but I am immediately drawn to the 1950s. The formal "Luncheon" leads us to believe that it was prior to 1970. I envision a chrome retro look with vinyl seating and the linoleum flooring so common in that era. Unpretentious and unassuming, we can perhaps imagine that Skelly's look was somewhat informal and "no frills," with the appeal of a large dining room but offering guests the warmth and friendliness of a small diner.

Meanwhile, the neighbors next door outfitted the public for the grandest of occasions. Beginning in 1959, the husband-and-wife team of William and June Sherkow ran this downtown location, one of seven stores they owned in the Milwaukee metropolitan area. Not unlike many family-owned businesses, they prided themselves on personalized and attentive service. They took their role seriously: to outfit the public for memorable and grand events and to satisfy their customers. William focused on managing the day-to-day operations. June handled the marketing, including advertising and corporate promotions, and staged fashion shows. Family friend and longtime employee Manie Katz contributed by attracting both new and repeat customers, as he had developed a reputation as "the Old Tux Fitter" with a big smile. Sadly, as the demand for formal wear declined in favor of more casual attire, the industry suffered significantly. The Sherkows sold the business in 1982 to Desmond's Formal Wear of La Crosse.

Skelly's and Sherkow's. When a parking structure was torn down a couple of years ago, the sign's presence downtown made it even more beautiful.

PRITZLAFF HARDWARE COMPANY

While at first glance this sign looks relatively unimpressive, what it signified during its prime was quite the contrary. Located at 143 West St. Paul, this street-level sign stating "Entrance to Shipping Dept." marked the location of Pritzlaff Hardware Company, founded by Prussian immigrant John C. Pritzlaff in 1850. While the structure is commonly referred to as the Pritzlaff Building, it is truly more of a complex. Each of the six Cream City brick buildings were constructed as Pritzlaff continued to expand his operations, the first of which in 1875 and the sixth having been completed in 1919. The shipping building faced north. The face of this seven-story building consists of five oversized windows on the ground level, each labeled with a number, starting at 3 and ending at 7. The bottom of the sign has an arrow pointing to the left, which is directly toward a corridor between the buildings.

Pritzlaff wisely sought out the location between West St. Paul and West Plankinton in downtown Milwaukee to build his behemoth distribution warehouse. Here, the transport of goods by rail and ship were facilitated by the nearly direct access to the Milwaukee River, feeding directly into Lake Michigan, and by proximity to the adjacent railroad tracks behind the building. Pritzlaff goods included housewares, hardware, paint, sporting goods, toys, auto parts and a wide variety of nearly anything and everything that was sold. It was a business-to-business operation, never selling directly to the consumer. During the rise in popularity of the mail-order catalogue, Pritzlaff displayed his products—thousands of them—in heavy, leather-bound catalogues, as opposed to lighter paperback catalogues offered by competitors. This simple action alone separated Pritzlaff from other distributors, demonstrating the commitment to exceed expectations by offering higher-quality products and exemplary service. Pritzlaff was certainly a force to be reckoned with in the industry.

While the buildings have been restored, renovated and repurposed, these alphabetical markings are a constant reminder of what once was. The Pritzlaff Building now hosts formal corporate events and elegant weddings and provides captivating photo-shoot backdrops: a stark contrast to the industrial warehouse that occupied these walls for over a century.

OPPOSITE The Pritzlaff Building went from an old hardware distribution center to one of Milwaukee's finest event venues. The building had quite the journey.

RITZ CAMERA

"Photofinishing Specialists for over 50 Years." This standard block print stenciled on an interior wall, despite its simplicity, holds great significance. Similar to the abandoned space it occupies in the once-thriving Grand Avenue Mall, photofinishing in its traditional form has nearly reached obsolescence due to the dominance of digital technologies. The former and last-known occupant of this space, Ritz Camera, was certainly a giant in the industry for decades.

Ritz Camera, founded by Benjamin Ritz, opened as a portrait studio in New Jersey in 1918. By 1936, Benjamin had expanded his operation into Washington, D.C., where he partnered with his brother Edward and ventured into photoprocessing. In the early 1980s, David Ritz, son of Edward, assumed leadership of operations. David implemented an aggressive growth strategy, most of which centered on acquisitions. Ritz Camera grew to be the largest retail camera and photo-imaging company in the United States in 2005.

However, while some attribute financial losses to poor management decisions and underperforming acquisitions, one cannot ignore the fact that consumer appetites for traditional cameras and printing changed with the rising popularity and availability of cellular phone cameras beginning in the middle of the first decade of the 2000s. The ever-expanding capability of photosharing and digital photofinishing features appealed to the typical customer as 2010 approached. Not surprisingly, Ritz Camera filed Chapter 11 bankruptcy in 2012.

I often struggle to remember how we ever managed before cellphones and digital cameras. As a child, I can recall the excitement of dropping off film at our local photo developer and the anticipation of what seemed like forever waiting for the photos. When the photos were finally ready, I habitually checked the number that developed, as this was typically handwritten on the front of the envelope. I recall the immense joy I felt during those rare moments when *every* single photo from a roll of film had been printed! Peeling back the flap of the envelope in wonderment was like opening a gift: How do they look? How many were blurry from not holding the camera still? How many photo subjects were obscured by my finger as it accidentally covered the lens? Future generations will never be able to experience the exhilaration of waiting for photos. I cherish those memories. This is not just another fading sign in an abandoned space: it represents the dying art that captured the memories of generations before us.

A former camera store at the Grand Avenue Mall. The mall is now going through a major transformation, and this area is being converted into apartments.

MILLER HIGH LIFE

Avert your eyes from the markings left by a local graffiti artist on the bottom outline of this sprawling sign. Nearly fading from existence, this ad originally encompassed the entire building façade.

At first glance, the most distinct words are near the bottom edge of the sign: "Food Market" and "Phone West 4520." It is likely that at one time these were two separate signs, the newer overlaying the older. The line of text following the food market lettering is almost completely illegible. It also looks as if a different font was used, which further supports the theory that these are two overlapping signs. Heavy winds, rain and vines, which have presumably damaged the surface for decades, have contributed to the overall decay. However, with an intent gaze and squinted eyes, one can see "Miller High Life Beer" over a red background comprising the top two-thirds of the sign.

Miller Brewing Company has consistently ranked in the top three of breweries nationwide and has battled for the number one position with Anheuser-Busch for decades. Originating from the Plank Road Brewery, Miller Brewing Company was founded in 1855 by Frederick Miller, who arrived from Germany with brewing knowledge and a secret, unique brewer's yeast in hand. Miller spent all but $1,000 of the $9,000 he had in his pocket on arriving in the United States with his wife, Josephine, and son, Joseph, for the Plank Road Brewery. Coincidentally, the Plank Road Brewery was owned by Frederick Charles Best, son of the Pabst Brewing company founder. In 1903, Miller High Life Beer launched, and it was named the "Champagne of Beers" for its effervescence, high quality and unique champagne-style bottles. The label portrayed what it marketed itself to be: "the high life." Embellished with gold trim, the label represented a pricier, higher-quality option than other competitor brands.

Little is known about the food market that was once here. The four-digit phone numbers preceded by a word were prominent between the 1920s and 1950s. We can presume, based on the extensive fading, that this was likely painted in the 1930s.

At the time of this writing, a revitalization project has been discussed for a section of the Concordia neighborhood, which has called for the demolition of this building. Fortunately, this image will preserve the essence of the once-popular neighborhood food markets, obsolete phone exchanges and sprawling painted beer ads.

This Miller High Life ghost sign was exposed decades ago on West Wisconsin Avenue after a Marc's Big Boy was demolished next to it. The land was never redeveloped, which makes the ghost sign easy to view.

LAACKE AND JOYS

This sign likely stirs up fond memories of many summer camping trips taken by Milwaukeeans. The crackling of the campfire flames, the pleasant aroma of burning firewood, the Coleman lantern that zapped insects all night, the s'mores! The dewy grass in the morning, the chill in the evening and the starry skies, with children enthusiastically searching for the North Star, the Large and Small Dippers and any other constellation they could find. Camping has always been a great pastime for many, as Wisconsin has a plethora of beautiful campgrounds, making for an affordable outdoor summer vacation. Many will recall this absurdly heavy Wildwood canvas tent, which was extremely labor-intensive to erect, containing stainless steel poles and connectors that somewhat resembled a set of tinker toys. Despite the challenges with the assembly, once the tent was in place, the campers inside were protected from the chill of a brisk night, and the tent was secure enough to remain intact during heavy winds.

Laacke and Joys were formed in 1957 by way of the merger between the R. Laacke Company and the Joys Brothers. Laacke and Joys filed for a U.S. trademark registration of the Wildwood name on September 25, 1975. It was a premier shopping establishment for camping and sporting goods of all varieties, and the Wildwood tent could be spotted on every campground in the 1970s and '80s. The location of this sign, at 1433 North Water Street, was the showroom and lone location from 1961 until 2013. The building has since been demolished, which sealed the fate for the sign as well.

OPPOSITE Wildwood Tents. The former Laacke and Joys complex went through renovations in 2016. When the façade was removed, the original sign was revealed.

HOTEL WISCONSIN

Hotel Wisconsin broke ground in 1912 and officially opened its doors in 1913. Undergoing an expansion before opening, the hotel boasted five hundred guest rooms and was marketed as a "luxury" property. The interior, while not displaying the grandeur of the Pfister Hotel a few blocks away, possessed charm and beauty. Retail space on the main levels included a variety of shops and services, including a tailor shop, a coffee shop and a shoe store (to name a few). The Hotel Wisconsin also had multiple dining rooms, each with its own character: the Colonial, Badger and Circus Rooms, and the Blackamoor Cocktail Lounge. In 1987, a cabaret-themed restaurant, Café Melange, occupied space here for ten years. Hotel Wisconsin enjoyed fabulous success for many years and hosted national performing acts and politicians, including First Lady Eleanor Roosevelt, throughout its tenure. It enjoyed many remarkable years before closing in 2003.

From the time I remember it, which was in the mid-1980s, Hotel Wisconsin appeared to be a neglected and somewhat "seedy" joint. It had an ominous appearance: dark and brooding with a gabled roof and institutional-style windows. It looked more like a depressing and aged apartment building than a hotel. The sign, which is located on the lower side of the building, points toward Old World Third Street and is probably the brightest spot on the entire dingy exterior, contrasted in sunny yellow and red. The glory days of the Hotel Wisconsin, while ending decades earlier, came to a complete halt when it was sold in 1997. The hotel ceased operations entirely in 2003.

The structure is now a renovated apartment complex, and the sign remains and reminds us of a hotel that in its prime was a bustling establishment that attracted thousands weekly and was revered as one of the more luxurious hotel properties in Milwaukee.

ABOVE Hotel Wisconsin. The perfect pop of color appears on this ghost sign in a downtown alley. It's in perfect condition.

STEINMEYER WHOLESALE GROCERY

The sign is simplistic, yet it articulates clearly the establishment being advertised and the line of business it operates. What is most appealing about this ad is not the content or design itself but how the ad survived a renovation. Lettering is obscured by the newly constructed floor and ceiling. The upper portion of the top row of letters has been completely cut off by the wood plank ceiling. However, you can see "Wm Steinmeyer," followed by the second and third lines of "Groceries and Wine." To the left, vertically written and also cut off, is the name "Steinmeyer."

The Steinmeyer building was erected in 1893; in 1974, it was designated a Wisconsin historical landmark. William Steinmeyer, of German descent, was a successful businessman and prominent grocer who, in 1865, established Steinmeyer Wholesale Grocery. He managed the operations until his death

William Steinmeyer Grocery.

in 1892 and, unfortunately, never saw the completion of this Romanesque Revival block building that he commissioned. William's brother, Charles, and son-in-law, Emil Ott, oversaw the conclusion of the building's construction and continued with the business until 1940. They specialized in home food deliveries, common before supermarkets came into favor after World War II.

At the time of this writing, the Steinmeyer building is home to the Wisconsin Cheese Mart on the ground level. This sign is located on the fifth floor, which has been converted from an expansive warehouse into repurposed office space. The new owners have graciously pledged to leave this vital sign intact.

SEN-SEN BREATH MINTS

It is all a façade! And it truly is. On first viewing this grandiose sign, which scales the entire north side of the Broadway Theatre Center at 158 North Broadway, the first question that enters the mind is, "Why?" Why so large, extending nearly six stories? Why here at this location? Why such a massive advertisement for a breath mint? All are valid questions regarding this painted advertisement for Sen-Sen, a popular breath mint invented by Thomas Dunn and distributed by the company bearing his name. The two main ingredients were licorice and anise, an atypical flavor profile compared to the peppermint, cinnamon and spearmint varieties we are accustomed to. Logic would dictate that there must have been a pharmacy or five-and-dime located here at one time. Alternatively, perhaps the Thomas Dunn Company invested in painted advertisements in major cities during the mint's popularity.

However, logic is overruled in this instance. This is a fake ghost sign. This Sen-Sen sign was painted as part of a backdrop on the set of the 1969 film *Gaily, Gaily*, a comedy set in 1910 Chicago starring Beau Bridges and Margot Kidder. I find it incredulous that the side of a building was allowed to become permanently altered. Why had they not used a temporary backdrop, instead of applying the lead-based paint, which is costly and time-consuming and poses health risks? The sign was restored in 1993.

ABOVE Sen-Sen. "Feelin' hoarse? Grab some Sen-Sen!" This sign was created for a movie filmed fifty years ago in the Historic Third Ward.

AB DICK COPYING

Even with limited information and only several lines of text, it is possible to unravel the mystery behind faded signs. Based on lettering font and references to services, we can often conclude what may have been.

Trying to decipher the remains of this sign is like putting together pieces of a puzzle. In the East Town neighborhood at 770 North Milwaukee Street we find a sign that has faded considerably despite being one of the newest signs in this book. This is ironic, since this sign advertised printing and copying services. Based on the typescript, this ad was likely painted in the 1980s.

The first line begins "AB." What can be surmised from this is that it must have at one time read "AB DICK," as this was one of the largest printing press and office supply manufacturers and distributors in the United States. The second line reads "Copying," while the third line has wholly vanished.

The next two lines provide a few more clues, as they indicate a business name—the letters "Rob" are followed by a very faint "E." The remainder of the word is obscured. What we know is that this building was at one time home to Robertson's Printing, supplier of graphic arts materials, a distributor and servicer of printing presses and a provider of copy and production services.

Scuffed, yet legible, the fifth line reads "Authorized Distributor." AB Dick, a Chicago-based company established in 1883, was one of the world's largest manufacturers of mimeograph and xerographic equipment during the bulk of the twentieth century. Even though the company was acquired by the British General Electric Company in 1979, the business still operated under the AB Dick name.

The earliest documented tenant of this building was the Milwaukee Tile and Mosaic Company, which resided here for at least ten years between the 1940s and '50s. In the early 1950s, AB Printing assumed occupancy.

I can only imagine that at one time Robertson's enjoyed great success servicing businesses not only in downtown Milwaukee but also in nearby suburbs. We do not know if it was retirement or pressure to keep pace with the intense competition from national chains, many of which were founded in the 1980s, that led to Robertson's demise. It's more certain that as rapidly as this sign is disappearing, Robertson's Printing is slowly fading from the memory of Milwaukeeans.

AB...
COPYING
...
ROB...
AUTHORIZED DISTRIBUTO...

Robertson's Printing Supplies.
This sign is fading pretty
quickly. It was more legible just
a couple of years ago.

THE AMBASSADOR HOTEL

When looking at this photo of the Ambassador Hotel, it is the grand, eye-catching neon sign, standing bold and proud against the horizon, that steals one's attention. What else do you notice? Shift your gaze downward, and you will spot severely faded script reading "Ambassador Hotel," presumably painted during the hotel's earlier days. Rapidly deteriorating, the first five letters of "Ambassador" are nearly illegible, as is "Hotel."

Established in 1928, the Ambassador Hotel is adorned with the splendor and grandiosity of the decade in which it was designed: marble floors, decorative wainscoting, nickel sconces, elegant chandeliers, bronze elevators and the characteristic geometric shapes that symbolized the Art Deco style that swept the United States and Europe in the 1920s and '30s. Straight out of a scene in *The Great Gatsby*, the Ambassador Hotel emanates sophistication and wealth. Retaining the glamour of a bygone era, the Ambassador grants all who pass through the front lobby the opportunity to experience life through the eyes of guests decades ago.

OPPOSITE Ambassador Hotel. One ghost outside, many ghosts inside. This hotel is one of Milwaukee's gems, and its history is fascinating.

GOLL AND FRANK CO.

A spectacular ghost sign spans the Milwaukee skyline, clearly visible to all passersby from the Interstate 794 East-West Freeway. Standing seven stories high, the Merchandise Building at 301 North Water Street is home to arguably one of the more recognizable signs in this collection. Located directly on the Milwaukee River and just south of East St. Paul Avenue, the building officially lies in the Third Ward. The ad has held up well, considering that, at the time of this photo, the age is projected to be at least eighty-five years old. The sign reads "Goll & Frank Co.—Wholesale Distributors—Notions and Furnishings—Goods." Looking closer at the second line, we can presume that, at one time, part or all of this sign was once restored—judging from faint remnants of previous lettering twice the font size underneath the smaller yet bolder print.

Young German immigrants Julius Goll and August Frank started their distribution and trade business in 1852. They sold everything from linens to hardware, from clothing to housewares. They worked excessively long hours while pouring their heart and soul into the company. Frank at one time reportedly said, "Business is so good at present that I hardly know where my head is from seven in the morning until nine at night. I have to gulp my food down, and there is hardly time to caress my wife and child."

Years of hard work paid off. By 1864, the business had grown exponentially, expanding its customer base to Iowa and Minnesota. Having outgrown their former facility, they built a much larger building at 301 North Water Street. Situated ideally near significant roadways, waterways and railways, the new location was a wise choice. Goods could be transported seamlessly with ease and efficiency. By 1882, the company had grown to forty-four employees, consisting of warehouse workers and salesmen.

Tragically, the Great Fire of 1892 destroyed much of the original building. While not as large in scale as the Great Fire of Chicago some twenty years earlier, this blaze caused sheer devastation throughout much of the Third Ward, displacing nearly 1900 residents and destroying more than 440 buildings spanning a sixteen-block radius. Having to rebuild once again, Goll and Frank hired famed architecture firm Ferry and Clas to erect this impressive seven-story building in 1896. Listed in the National Register of Historic Places, the structure was stylized as Romanesque Revival, graced with arches, columns and a grand exterior entrance.

Business continued to flourish into the twentieth century. However, between 1922 and 1929, the partnership between Goll and Frank began to dissolve. Goll continued to manage dry goods; Frank managed notions. In 1929, company president Frederick Goll, son of Julius, renamed the business Fred T. Goll and Sons. This signified the end of the relationship between Goll and Frank, as ownership had transferred to Frederick and his two sons, Julius and Harry. In 1938, seven years after Frederick's passing, the name changed once again to the J.H. Goll Company. In the final transition, the company narrowed its focus to linens and changed the name for the last time to J.H. Goll Company Linens. This venture continued for less than a decade and ceased all operations in the 1940s.

The sign, though fading, provides a chance to pause and reflect: two young and ambitious men, starting with nothing, built a small empire with nothing but determination and hard work. They were regarded as two of the most successful entrepreneurs of their time.

ABOVE Groll and Frank. One of the largest ghost signs in downtown Milwaukee. It's hard to miss when you're on the corner of Water Street and St. Paul Avenue.

PETERS DRY CLEANERS AND LAUNDRY

Lying on the outskirts of Westown just west of the Marquette University campus, we stumble across Peters Dry Cleaners and Laundry. The Peters family has owned and operated dry cleaners throughout the Milwaukee area, and this particular location has been open since 1927. This vibrant sign has been restored in recent years and sits where drivers on Interstate 94 have an unobstructed view of it. The neatly pressed and colorful array of shirts and ties exemplifies the quality of work provided. The Peters name stands proudly at the helm of the sign, with a slightly angled letter "P" enveloped by two strands of wheat. Numerous signs in Milwaukee have been designed with wheat sheaves to symbolize beer. While the wheat symbol has no relevance in the dry-cleaning industry, it has been synonymous with success and prosperity. And the Peters family enjoyed that for nearly a century.

Peters Dry Cleaners. How can you not drop off your dry cleaning here? There's a ghost sign!

3

NORTH SIDE

Near the end of the nineteenth century, as the population of Milwaukee continued to grow, residential and commercial development expanded outside of downtown. The North Side, much like the rest of the city, was first settled by German immigrants. More than a dozen neighborhoods constitute the North Side, the first of which were on the outskirts of downtown and included the Harambee, Williamsburg Heights and Brewer's Hills neighborhoods. The architecture reflects that which was common near the turn of the century, with an abundance of Queen Anne, Polish flat, Victorian and Italianate structures. Duplexes were constructed almost on a par with single-family homes during this period, reflective of the economic struggles faced by Americans in the early twentieth century. As more neighborhoods developed following World War II, Cape Cod and Craftsman single-family homes began to dominate the housing market. Near the time of the Great Depression, Polish and Italian immigrants began to flood into the North Side neighborhoods, followed closely by African Americans during the Great Migration from the South. By the 1970s, African Americans were, and remain today, the dominant ethnic/racial group in most North Side neighborhoods.

GETTELMAN'S BREWERY

Located at 124 West Keefe, this beauty resides in the Williamsburg Heights neighborhood. At the time of this writing, the building is occupied by a childcare center. Most painted ads featured the typical shades of white and gray painted over the original brick façade. This painter chose to use vibrant shades of red, orange and yellow. Perhaps it is trying to say, "I may not be as mighty as other breweries, but I am equally as important and impressive!" The sign is striking and attention-grabbing. What remains is approximately one-fourth of the original, based on what appears to have been a circle or oval enveloping the Gettelman name.

The original ad was painted over a dark gray background directly on the red-brick façade. It appears that a billboard of sorts once hung over the original Gettelman's ad and that the blue paint had been applied around it. At one time, this building most likely operated as a tavern on the main level, with the owner residing on the upper level.

Gettelman's Brewery was one of several top breweries in Milwaukee. George Schweickhart, a German immigrant from Mühlhausen, Alsace, formed Menomonee Brewery in 1856, presumptively based on the brewery's location just west of the Menomonee River Valley. In 1871, Adam Gettelman, George's son-in-law, became a partner in the brewery. Adam became the sole proprietor in 1887 and thus changed the name to A. Gettelman Brewing Company. While the brewery was at the forefront in the industry, such as pioneering the design of the first steel keg in 1933 and being the first American brewery to import beer from Germany. In 1959, Gettelman's was rendered unable to compete with Pabst, Schlitz, Miller and the other brewing empires at the time. As a result, Miller Brewing purchased A. Gettelman Brewing in 1961 and continues to carry "Milwaukee's Best," the last carryover from Gettleman's.

OPPOSITE Gettelman Brewing Company. This is one of the most colorful ghost signs in Milwaukee. It's easy on the eyes, and the colors pop.

ADAM SCHROTH

Horse-drawn carriages, also known as "buggies," were one of the primary modes of transportation in the nineteenth century and through the early twentieth. They were accessible to the middle and upper classes of society, increasing in elegance and design the higher the family's stature in society. However, even the wealthiest individuals often did not have a carriage large enough to appropriately honor their recently deceased loved ones in funeral processions or to celebrate joyous newlyweds. Enter Adam Schroth.

Schroth was a German-born gentleman who immigrated to the United States in 1854. After deciding to make Milwaukee his home, following the suit of many other Germans during this period, he found and married a suitable bride, who gave birth to a son in 1861. Adam carried forth the skills and traditions from his homeland by pursuing his love of baking and confectionery. Adam's firstborn son, Adam L., followed in his father's footsteps, learning and honing the baking trade from his father. He briefly took this trade to Johnson Brothers Baking Company, where he was employed as a salesman. However, in 1888, the younger Adam abruptly pursued an alternative career path and became an undertaker. His wife, referred to as "Lady Undertaker," worked alongside him. In the 1895 business directory, Adam is also associated with a business partner named Joseph Zander located at 509 North Broadway. It is unclear how long this partnership lasted and when the business moved to the current location.

The sign, located at 1938 Vel R. Phillips Avenue in Halyard Park, is partially cut off due to white siding installed decades later. Today, this sits on the north-facing wall of the Francis Center, partially obscured by foliage when in bloom. It is surprising that this sign has endured the tattering of rain, snow, and high winds over what we can surmise as more than one hundred years. Oddly, there are no records beyond 1920 supporting the idea that the business was in operation at this location, or at all. There is no indication that the sign had been restored throughout the years. All of the letterings, albeit fading, are legible today:

ADAM SCHROTH
UNDERTAKER
CARRIAGES
FOR FUNERALS AND WEDDINGS

We can surmise that Adam L. Schroth was well known in the neighborhood, touching the lives of nearly every family through one or both of these ceremonies at one time or another. His carriages were elegant, meticulously maintained and reserved only for events such as to celebrate new beginnings or the endings of life. The funeral carriages provided by Adam Schroth were built perfectly for the average sized casket, which was protected from the elements and displayed through a glass enclosure.

The horse-drawn carriage and its place in these traditions fell out of favor with the rising popularity of automobiles and hearses. As most in the wedding and funeral business will verify, demand is always steady. But Adam may not have anticipated the progress of the automobile, which would render his carriage services obsolete. Adam L. passed away in 1936 at the age of seventy-six.

ABOVE Adam Schroth. Funerals and weddings—pretty much covers it all. They get you coming and going, but they're the last person to let you down.

J.C. DEFFNER/VAN HOUTEN'S COCOA

One has to strain to read this one. It is fading badly, which is attributable to the age of the sign. This beautiful, Italianate commercial building dates back to 1885.

On the north side of the Deffner Building, at 2036 North Dr. Martin Luther King Drive in the Brewer's Hill neighborhood, "Harness Maker—Repairing Done on Short Notice" is written inside the border of the upper sign, followed by "Van Houten's Cocoa" encompassing the lower half of the wall. The bottom line, obscured by bushes, reads "Best and Goes Farthest," the tagline for Van Houten's Cocoa.

As I close my eyes, what pops into my head are images of a bygone era: men in suits with top hats and women in a long dresses and bonnets. Nobody worked on Sunday. Everyone knew their neighbors. And trains, streetcars and horse-pulled buggies were the primary forms of transportation.

A gentleman by the name of J.C. Deffner, a harness maker and dealer of horse goods, for whom the building was erected in 1885, operated his business here. The building is a wonder in itself—a beautiful Victorian Italianate, commercial, two-story edifice. With pressed metal cornices, cast-iron columns and detailed brickwork, it is an architectural beauty. Deffner, a native of Bavaria, was a respected businessman in his day. I also suspect that he and Schroth (see the previous photo) were associates, as their properties were only two-tenths of a mile from each another. Alas, J.C. passed away in 1913, and we can presume the business died with him.

This sign has seen an incredible amount of progress over more than one hundred years—both socially and culturally. I can only presume that harness making was a lucrative endeavor at the time, much like the auto mechanic of today. The sign remains barely intact as a reminder of a time before life as we know it. We can live a sliver of that life when we reserve a horse-driven carriage for special events. While this may seem glamorous to us, keep in perspective that life was not at all luxurious in those bygone times.

The uppermost sign refers to the flagship product from Coenraad Van Houten, a Dutch-born inventor of the cocoa press (patented in 1828). Van Houten was responsible for popularizing cocoa drinks by cultivating a more edible and soluble form due to his unique pressing method. At the turn of the twentieth century Van Houten's was a top-ten U.S. brand.

When we study the two signs, the fading and the lettering style could lead us to conclude that these signs were painted, if not at the same time,

very close in time. However, unless there was a second tenant alongside J.C. Deffner, it is doubtful that cocoa was served and sold with a custom-made harness! The building has a triple-bay storefront, so it is entirely possible that another tenant occupied this space alongside Deffner. Another theory is that the sign was sponsored by Van Houten's directly, as part of its marketing efforts. Much of Van Houten's international success was due to effective marketing and extensive targeted campaigns, particularly during this time. It has been challenging to find any documentation about who the tenant was that would have commissioned this painted ad, whether it was a chocolatier or a five-and-dime owner. Moreover, city records have produced little information about any of the occupants following the death of Deffner. Unsubstantiated rumors and speculation have pointed to the operation as a brothel in the 1980s. At the time of this writing, the Northern Chocolate Company, established in 1991, is the primary occupant of the building.

ABOVE Deffner Harnesses and Van Houten's Cocoa. Some ghost signs creep around corners, but they're harmless.

STEREO CABINETS

This sign, painted at 2228 West Fond du Lac Avenue, resides on a dilapidated building that likely was quite captivating at its peak. We can see clearly only a few words: "Cabinets," "AM-FM" and a price, "$599." Seeing this brings a smile to my face, as it triggers lovely childhood memories of my grandparents' house. The centerpiece in the dining room was not the table, but instead a large, beautifully polished, wood stereo cabinet. It was embellished with intricately carved patterns with fleur-de-lis, scrolls and other ornamental trims. The unit contained built-in speakers, a turntable, a storage area and an AM/FM radio, which was quite a luxury at that time. More than the television, this was my grandparents' prime source of entertainment: listening to radio shows and news broadcasts while also having the ability to listen to their favorite records when the radio signed off for the evening. It opened on the top, so when the lid closed, it looked like a typical cabinet that blended in with the rest of the furniture. As a child, I didn't think much of it, but as an adult, I can now appreciate the enormous investment in these major decorative yet practical items so prevalent in midcentury homes.

Based on the architecture and the age of other buildings in the neighborhood, this building may have been constructed in the early 1900s. The sign itself is severely damaged, which may have been partially caused by (although not shown in this photo) the overgrowth of trees and shrubbery scuffing the paint. For this three-story building, the top two floors appear to be residential units, with a ground-level storefront. Unfortunately, there is little documentation on this property and the business that once resided here.

OPPOSITE AM-FM & TV Consoles. This is from a time when ghost signs advertised AM/FM radios and TV consoles and cabinets.

DEL LAMB

Outside of the western perimeter of the Metcalfe Park neighborhood, bordered on the north and south by Center Street and North Avenue and on the east and west from Twentieth to Thirty-Fifth Streets, we find the former location of Del Lamb Sport Shop. Milwaukee native Del (Delbert) Lamb was a two-time Winter Olympian, having competed in the 1936 and 1948 games. He was also an inductee into the National Speed Skating Hall of Fame. After retiring from the sport following the 1948 Olympics, Del chose to pursue an alternative avenue that would allow him to share his love of sports of all sorts with others: he opened a sporting-goods store.

This ad is in relatively good condition and reads "All Type of Sports Equipment—Del Lamb Sport Shop—Bicycles—Hobbies—Hunting—Fishing—Specializing in Ice Skates—Bicycles Repaired."

Del Lamb operated the shop from 1948 to 1958. I wonder if those who pass and gaze on this painted ad truly recognize and appreciate who Delbert Lamb was—a man of tremendous accomplishment with a pervasive passion for sports and fitness.

RIGHT Del Lamb Sport Shop. A favorite place to stop in the neighborhood to get skates sharpened and to purchase a bicycle.

MILWAUKEE SOAP

Nestled in a residential neighborhood along the 30th Street Industrial Corridor, we find "Milwaukee Soap" in a small section on an exterior wall in an otherwise sprawling industrial complex. A large commercial building that looks like it had at one time been a factory or a warehouse, it sits abandoned today and is located on Thirty-First and Galena. It does appear that the sign at one time spread downward in alignment with the adjacent block windows. It appears that there was another word, or possibly a price, painted below the word "Soap." It has completely worn off, so it is difficult to speculate what may have once been there.

There is little concrete and documented information on Milwaukee Soap, but we do know that it dates back to the 1960s. Before Milwaukee Soap, Wisconsin Ice and Coal was a tenant for many decades and may have been the original occupant of the warehouse. City directory research points to the fact that, during the 1950s, the warehouse may have been subdivided and leased to multiple businesses. A firm named Esser Wholesaler is listed as the primary tenant in the 1960s. Was Milwaukee Soap perhaps managed under this wholesaler?

Supposedly, there were multiple retail locations throughout the Milwaukee metro area, yet it is unclear if this was also a retail outlet or if this was exclusively a packaging and assembly plant. Another piece of the puzzle not yet unraveled is whether Milwaukee Soap manufactured its own products, operated as retail only representing "seconds" of major brands at bargain prices, did both—or did none of the above. Customers recount that they were told "Milwaukee Soap had no affiliation with any other companies in the industry." That would then leave one to conclude that Milwaukee Soap did indeed produce its own line of soap products. The company is reported to have been founded in 1931, but, again, it has been a struggle to uncover what little documentation exists about Milwaukee Soap. It makes me wonder, with the lack of marketing and advertising in general, if it operated somewhat covertly. Was the advertising exclusively "word of mouth?"

The only concrete evidence that can be verified is based on the relished accounts from numerous Milwaukee residents. Former patrons, who were children at the time, recall memories of shopping with a mother or grandmother, and they reflect with a smile about the massive amounts of soap they would load into the car. There are stories of "annual pilgrimages" to Milwaukee Soap to purchase dozens upon dozens of boxes, bags or bars

of powdered laundry detergent, body soap and dish soap. Reportedly, all of the products were unlabeled, unbranded and absurdly inexpensive. The packaging was simple, with all items in plain wrapping with generic labels such as "soap" or "detergent." Milwaukee Soap was an incredible bargain for the savvy shopper who wanted no frills and no fuss and who desired economy over anything else.

Thousands of teenage newspaper carriers laid their eyes on this sign nearly every day after school in the 1960s and 1970s. The *Milwaukee Journal*, before it was the *Journal Sentinel* under *USA Today* ownership, was at one time the afternoon newspaper subscribed to by the majority of Milwaukee households. A station where newspapers were assembled and divided into carriers' routes stood directly across from the Milwaukee Soap sign.

This sign, fading fast, leaves behind a mystery.

ABOVE Milwaukee Soap. Walking the tracks through this corridor is interesting. Milwaukee Soap was an original and the oldest detergent outlet.

PIEHLER CIGAR COMPANY

"La Palina—The Quality Cigar. Popular Because Best." The ideas are simply stated in bold, white block lettering on a painted black canvas. Despite peeling, the lettering is still distinct and clear. This Piehler Cigar Company sign was recently unveiled when adjacent housing was torn down in favor of a new parking lot. Obstructed for decades by neighboring houses, this gem has been incredibly well preserved. Dating back to as early as 1908, Piehler Cigar Company was one of dozens of smoke shops and distributors in the city.

Taking a closer look at the sign, note that, on the bottom right of the sign in small, capitalized block print are the words "Steller Signs." We can draw the likely conclusion that Edward Steller, a sign painter who lived a few blocks from this location, was commissioned to paint this for Piehler. He was listed as a proprietor for American Wallpaper and Paint Company in 1895. Of the painted signs remaining in the city today, this is the only Steller sign in this collection. We can also assume that this sign was painted at the turn of the twentieth century.

Sam Paley, a Ukrainian immigrant, opened the Congress Cigar Company in 1896 and launched La Palina as his first cigar, named after his wife, Goldie. La Palina translates to "The Paley." The cigar was wrapped with a gold foil label and decorated with the striking profile of Goldie, his beautiful wife. Much like Goldie herself, the cigar projected luxury and prestige. Pricier than others, La Palina was targeted at those who desired to project an image of prestige and preference for high standards and quality.

City records are inconsistent and difficult to obtain before and after the turn of the century. The operation dates of Piehler Cigar are therefore unknown. We do know that Columbia Savings Bank, which opened in 1924, resided in this building at 2000 West Fond du Lac Avenue for most of the twentieth century. We can safely ascertain that this sign was painted between 1908 and 1920 and that Piehler Cigar may have been in operation for approximately twenty years.

OPPOSITE Piehler Cigar Company/La Palina. Quite possibly the oldest ghost sign in Milwaukee, it's more than 110 years old and still preserved nicely.

MILWAUKEE WOOL CARDING

The textile industry was booming in the city throughout the late 1800s and well into the late 1900s. Milwaukee Wool Carding, shown here, was established by Adam Weingandt in 1883. Records indicate that Charles Weingandt, Adam's son, took control of the business at some point in the early 1920s. Located on the south side of the building at 2245 West Fond du Lac Avenue, this is a direct neighbor to the north of the AM/FM sign discussed earlier in this chapter.

The first line, obscured and damaged by a black, tar-like roofing substance, still clearly reads "Wool Carding Mills," followed by the words "H.C. Weingandt." Enveloped inside a rectangular border is very clear writing, as if it had been recently restored: "Wool Batts, Wool Carding, Feather Renovating Pillows, Pads, Quilts, Rug Shampooing." The bottom line reads, "Wool Quilts Made to Order."

Immediately beneath the sign lies the signature of Gordon F. Brenner, a professional sign painter. Little information about him and his business exists, except that he was born at the turn of the twentieth century. However, based on the condition of the sign and the age of Mr. Brenner, it is probable that this was painted no earlier than the 1940s.

Erected in 1925, this two-story Mediterranean Revival structure has the standard ground-floor storefront, presumably with residential quarters on the second floor. Two bricks grace the building façade: one dated 1883 and the other 1925. On the left, the brick imprinted with "1883" represents the inception of the business; the brick on the right indicates the erection of the current structure in 1925.

Building fires were devastating and, sadly, a common occurrence during these times, claiming many human casualties and destroying buildings and land in the process. While we do not know exactly what happened to the original 1883 property, we do know that this was the second and final home of Milwaukee Wool Carding.

There is little to no information about the business beyond 1940. This building is now home to the Friendship Club, which provides a welcoming and supportive sanctuary for those coping with alcohol and drug addiction.

OPPOSITE H.C. Weingandt was a business where people in town got their quilts made and took their wool to be cleaned.

4

SOUTH SIDE

Milwaukee's South Side can broadly be defined as the area south of downtown. Excluding many suburbs, some of the more well-known neighborhoods on the South Side include Bay View, Mitchell Street, Layton Park, Jackson Park and Lincoln Village. For this book, the Walker's Point neighborhood on the South Side has an entire dedicated chapter due to the plethora of signs in this heavily industrialized area.

If you ask a native Milwaukeean to explain where the South Side is, many will at some point in their explanation make reference to the "Polish side of town." History will support that statement. The South Side was heavily settled by the Poles as early as 1850 in various specialized and general labor occupations such as grocers, butchers, shoemakers, laborers, tavernkeepers and farmers, to name a few. The majority of Milwaukee's Polish population indeed settled in the area just south of Greenfield Avenue. Between 1890 and 1915, the population tripled to reach more than 100,000 Polish settlers alone.

When driving through the South Side today, one can still see the elaborate churches built in and around the turn of the century by Polish residents as they maintained robust ties and devotion to the Catholic Church. Some of these churches, including the Basilica of St. Josaphat, still integrate traditional Polish hymns and prayers into the Mass. Inarguably, the South Side maintains some of the most striking and beautiful churches in the city of Milwaukee. In the 1950s, many of Milwaukee's Poles, while remaining on the South Side, relocated farther southeast and southwest as the post–World War II economic boom spurred business and residential development into the southern suburbs. Today, the South Side is less Polish than it was a century ago, as the area is becoming increasingly diversified with a growing population of African Americans, Asian Americans, Mexican Americans, Central Americans and Puerto Ricans.

SEALTEST ICE CREAM

Our photo journey begins on the perimeter of the south side of "downtown" in the working-class suburb of West Allis. This fascinating ad, painted on the side exterior wall facing a parking lot, is located at 6780 West Lincoln Avenue. The building is a simple, single-story commercial structure with an unusual façade: a combination of red terra-cotta brick and Lannon stone (so named because it was discovered in Lannon, Wisconsin).

Here we find an interesting painted ad for Sealtest Ice Cream facing a parking lot. The blue painted canvas background was probably originally much brighter and more vivid than how it shows today. The words "Sealtest Ice Cream" are visible in the forefront inside of the center red section of the sign. But what does the sign below, in the faded blue, mean? It may read "Luick Dairy." On the right side vertically aligned, the word "Vitamins" can still be seen, despite the now-complete absence of the letters "V" and "S." Did a pharmacy at one time occupy this space? Without city records confirming this, it is a probable assumption.

Wisconsin, aptly named the "Dairy State," is one of the largest producers of dairy products in the United States. It is not surprising to find an ice cream distributor and warehouse just outside of downtown Milwaukee. What makes this sign interesting is that it appears that, when Sealtest was acquired by Luick Dairy in 1929, the existing Luick Dairy sign was simply painted over with the new Sealtest brand. While it may seem careless to not invest the time in removing the formerly painted sign before painting the new one, it is essential to remember that the majority if not all of the paint used in this period was lead-based. Used to enhance durability and protection against the elements, lead paint is difficult and tedious to remove, notwithstanding the health risks it presents in the process. Without conclusive data to support this assumption, based on the fading of the sign and history of the two businesses, we can presume that the original Luick sign was painted in the 1920s, followed closely by the second sign in the 1930s.

OPPOSITE Sealtest Ice Cream was the first dairy in the country to offer take-home ice cream. On a hot day, who wouldn't want some Sealtest Ice Cream?

CAMPIONE BAKERY

Close your eyes for just a moment. Now, imagine the aromas of garlic and fresh-baked bread wafting in the air. I don't know about you, but I cannot find much of anything more mouthwatering than the smell of freshly baked garlic bread, pizza and, well, anything Italian. Joe and Angie Campione, formerly of Brooklyn, relocated to Milwaukee, where they opened a bakery specializing in stone oven–baked Italian goods.

If you drive past this one quickly, you will undoubtedly miss it. Located on the second story and the side of this residential-commercial hybrid building, this painted ad is partially obstructed by a neighboring property and mature tree. In fading block print, the first letters in both "Campione" and "Bakery" were probably originally a truer hue of red, while the succeeding letters are green—the two dominant colors of the Italian flag.

Joseph Campione opened his first bakery in 1960 in the vibrant Italian neighborhood of Brady Street. Initially, it supplied Italian bread to local grocery stores and was quite successful in doing so. This location, in Forest Home Hills on Milwaukee's South Side, was the result of growth from the original site.

However, an unexpected turn of events occurred in the 1980s, when their business started to decline due to the increasing prevalence and popularity of on-site grocery store bakeries. The Campione family nimbly shifted gears and, in 1985, ventured into the frozen food market. In this venue, Campione Bakery produces "Old World Italian" breads, from the traditional garlic bread to Texas toast, from ciabatta breads to breadsticks; everything is baked hearth-style.

Campione Bakery swiftly dominated the frozen garlic bread market. The shift had proven to be a wise business decision, and this location was abandoned shortly thereafter for a larger facility on the North Side to handle an ever-expanding customer base. By 1994, Campione Bakery had again outgrown its space and moved into a larger location in Oak Creek, three years before Joe passed away in 1997. Campione Bakery still operates at this location today.

OPPOSITE Campione Bakery had great Italian bread. The aroma was wonderful and is sorely missed.

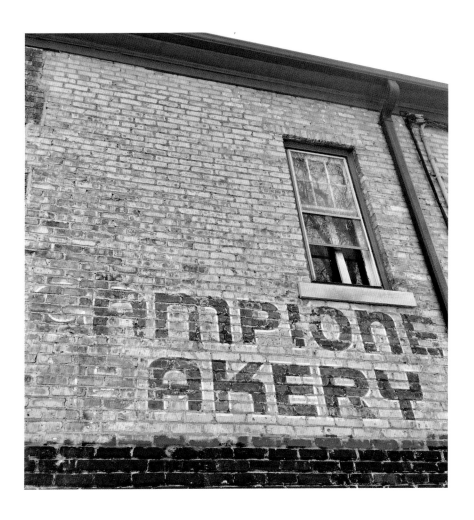

JAY'S

"Jay's—Can't Stop Eating 'Em." And you really couldn't! I remember as a child being so excited when my parents would return from the grocery store with the big white box engraved with the word "Jay's" scripted in white inside a bright blue circle. The chips were perfectly thin, adequately salted and addictive. Inside the standard box were two bags of chips, otherwise known as the "twin pak," ready to be devoured.

Here we find on this building at 3334 South Twenty-Seventh Street in the Southgate neighborhood a pervasively faded sign. The only reason I immediately recognized it was because of the childhood memory of the box! The emblem, off to the left, is hardly recognizable. Enclosed in a nearly invisible blue circle is the word "Jay's"; we can see remnants of the elegant cursive script, just as it had been displayed on the box. Only the first two words of the catchy marketing phrase "Can't Stop Eating 'Em," can be discerned on the right half of the sign. The red blur of paint above the Jay's symbol may have at one time read "Potato Chips." However, the decay is so extensive that one can only speculate.

Unlike most local establishments represented by ghost signs in the city, Jay's Chips was headquartered in Milwaukee's neighbor to the south, in the city of Chicago. Jay's enjoyed a healthy share of the snack market in Wisconsin, similar to other surrounding midwestern states like Minnesota, Indiana and Iowa.

A little-known fact is that Jay's was not named after anyone with a first or last name of "Jay." In 1929, the Japp family of Chicago embarked on what would grow into a multi-million-dollar subsidiary of Snyder's-Lance Foods, selling pretzels from the back of the family's truck. Leonard Sr. managed the business, while his wife, Eugenia, created a unique potato chip recipe that would soon take center stage over their pretzel operation. With the start of World War II and pervasive anti-Japanese sentiment, the name was changed from Mrs. Japp's Potato Chips to Jay's to avoid any negative connotations. With this handy information, we can conclude that the sign was posted after 1940; based on the fading, that decade seems probable.

OPPOSITE Jay's Potato Chips. I had to pull into a Taco Bell drive-through and buy a burrito to capture this ghost on South Twenty-Seventh Street. Not that I'm complaining.

BUD'S SPORT & MARINE

Without a doubt, Wisconsinites have an overwhelming love of the outdoors. The state boasts eighty thousand miles of streams and rivers, more than fifteen thousand lakes and over one thousand miles of shoreline between both Lake Michigan and Lake Superior. All combined, bodies of water in the state are home to approximately 150 species of fish. It should come as no surprise, with this abundant natural resource, that fishing and boating are favorite pastimes among locals, and both contribute significantly to Wisconsin tourism. This natural resource has been enjoyed and shared for generations. Wisconsinites will lovingly talk for hours about their cherished memories of time spent with parents and grandparents on the many waters throughout the state.

Probably greater than locals' love of catching fish is their love of consuming them. The "Friday Fish Fry" is a long-standing tradition and part of the culture in the state, more so than anywhere else in the United States. At any given time in Milwaukee—and pretty much any place in Wisconsin—there is a plethora of choices on Friday night. We can credit this tradition to the predominantly Roman Catholic Germans, Poles and other European groups that settled in Milwaukee over the years. There is no indication that this tradition will ever change. From supper clubs to German beer halls, from neighborhood pubs to family-owned restaurants, the tradition is pervasive throughout the city. Several Catholic churches prepare and serve a delicious and extremely affordable fish fry as a fundraising activity. Even more trendy and eclectic local restaurants serve their versions of a traditional fish fry, albeit with some modern twists. Cod and perch are most commonly served, but one can also find local, fresh-caught walleye and bluegills. The typical fish fry menu does not stray too far from the traditional fare, which includes delicately fried, beer-battered or grilled fish; marble rye bread; coleslaw; and a starch that could be anything from French fries or a baked potato to traditional German sides like German-style potato salad or potato pancakes with applesauce. In true Milwaukee style, a fish fry is not complete without a perfectly cold beer!

Adjacent to the city of Milwaukee perimeter lies the suburb of St. Francis, where we find this colorful and lively scene at 2918 East Layton Avenue. While the ad shows some signs of fading, this photo captured it in near-perfect condition. Painted on a bright, royal blue background representing a body of water, the red script lettering reads, "Bud's Sport and Marine Shop." Two

anglers in a small motorized fishing boat suitable for inland lakes and rivers are painted to the left. On the lower right, a banner reads, "Store & Display Room Straight Ahead to First Stop Light Then Right 4 Blocks." The store was located four blocks to the east on South Packard Avenue.

In 1946, Milton "Bud" Schmidt and his wife, Edith, opened Bud's Sport Shop, which operated until 1958. The name later changed to Bud's Sport & Marine, which is reflected on the sign here. Based on the theory that the name change occurred sometime after transfer of ownership, the sign was likely painted between 1960 and 1965. Bud's Sport & Marine appealed to the heart and soul of residents and their passion for sport and their equivalent love of the fish fry. Sadly, this vibrant sign has been removed.

ABOVE The Bud's Sport & Marine Shop sign was recently revealed after a building next door was torn down. The sign had been in hiding since the 1960s.

OLD HEIDELBERG BEER

This is a picture-perfect representation of a ghost sign that has nearly faded beyond recognition. It is located at 2988 South Kinnickinnic Avenue in Bayview, an artsy community on the southeast edge of Milwaukee. It is barely visible, and one has to focus intently to decipher the content. The ad itself is split between the brick façade closest to the front of the building in the original brown-clay brick and a whitewashed section closer to the rear. The latter portion is particularly undistinguishable.

Inside the black-bordered ad lies the word "Heidelberg" in a flourishing Germanic script, which appears to have been painted on top of a red banner. Encompassing the upper left, the word "Blatz" appears on a dark brown landscape. It is probable that the word "Old" was visible at one time before the word "Heidelberg," as this would have completed the brand name. The word "Beer" in block style is the most visible in the entire ad, near the bottom. What is intriguing about this sign is that if you look closely outside of the black-bordered section, you will find the word "Brew." This one word signifies one of those telltale hints that can help pinpoint the age of the sign.

Old Heidelberg Beer, produced under the Blatz name, used a formula that closely mimicked the classic German taste profile. In 1920, when Prohibition crippled breweries nationwide, the only option to remain viable was to produce alternative products. One of these was "brew," also referred to as "near beer." Essentially a nonalcoholic beer, these brews met the requirements provided by the U.S. government: any beverage produced was to contain less than 0.5 percent alcohol.

On the bottom edge in black, enveloped with a white border and lettering, the signature of "General Outdoor" is still quite visible. The General Outdoor Advertising Company formed in 1925 from a merger between the Fulton Group and the Cusack Company. Initially specializing in billboards and other outdoor posters, they eventually branched out into other forms of advertising, including neon signs and theater marquees. They had quite an impressive list of customers, representing both local market and major national brands, such as Coca-Cola, Du Pont, Johnson & Johnson and Wrigley's.

The clues in this sign support the idea that this ad was painted prior to the end of Prohibition in 1933 but after the inception of General Outdoor in 1925. Unless this one undergoes a restoration effort very soon, it will undoubtedly fade from existence.

A very old advertisement for Blatz and Old Heidelberg beer on the side of Lee's Luxury Lounge in Bay View.

MILWAUKEE SAUSAGE COMPANY

This red-brick processing plant was the final location for the Milwaukee Sausage Company, formed by Frank Spewachek. Frank emigrated from Bohemia with his family in 1890 as a teenager and settled in Milwaukee. He spent twenty years honing his skills in meat processing and production, working for local sausage producer L. Frank and Son. All the years of preparation paid off. In 1916, Frank partnered with Frank Klement to form their own production facility, the Milwaukee Sausage Company. Business flourished. In a few short years, they outgrew the original plant on Center Street, necessitating the relocation to 652 National Avenue. Continued expansion drove the need to move to their final location at 1334 West National Avenue, shown here.

The surname Klement is well known in the community. The sons of Frank Klement purchased Badger Sausage and formed Klement's Sausage in 1956. Klement's increased its public visibility with the institution of the "sausage races" in the early 1980s. Today, Klement's sausages can be found in the meat section of every grocery store in Milwaukee and throughout Wisconsin. The family of Frank Spewachek continued to manage the operations after Frank's death but finally closed the doors after more than sixty years in operation. In 2017, this sign was removed.

OPPOSITE Milwaukee Sausage Company opened in 1916 and enjoyed more than sixty years at 1334 West National Avenue. Unfortunately, the sign was painted over in 2017.

JOHN'S BARGAIN STORE/
BIG BEN'S SHOES

The Mitchell Street neighborhood, located on Mitchell Street between South Fifth and Fourteenth Streets, sits on the land previously owned and subdivided by Alexander Mitchell, a former U.S. senator and a prominent investor in the railroad and baking industries. Mitchell Street itself was named in 1857.

St. Stanislaus Church sits at the easternmost point of the Mitchell Street neighborhood. A spectacular Cream City brick cathedral on Fifth Street, St. Stanislaus proudly beckons visitors with its beauty. Erected in 1872, this landmark is the cornerstone of the Mitchell Street neighborhood and the first Polish-Catholic church in Milwaukee.

At one time, this predominantly Polish neighborhood buzzed with activity, shopping and restaurants, making it one of the most sought-after shopping districts in Milwaukee. Peppered with mom-and-pop stores and anchored by both local and national department stores such as Schuster's, Woolworth's and Goldmann's, Milwaukee residents from near and far flocked to this lively shopping mecca.

Envision yourself on Mitchell Street in the 1950s amid the hustle and bustle. The Polish language was pervasive, significantly overshadowing English. Everything you possibly needed or desired could be found at your fingertips. There were several restaurants in the area, including the famous lunch counter at Goldmann's. Customers arrived early and stayed late, making this an all-day adventure. The stores were packed with customers, and the crowds seemed never-ending.

By the early 2000s, the demographics had shifted dramatically. By then, about 75 percent of residents identified as Hispanic. Today, Spanish has replaced Polish in the neighborhood and is equally heard with English.

I vividly recall the emptiness and vacancies while walking down Mitchell Street as a teenager in the 1980s. With the popularity of shopping malls in the suburbs peaking in this decade, the area resembled a ghost town—an unfortunate downturn from the shopping haven it had once been. At the time of this writing, the neighborhood is undergoing an exciting revitalization, with much of the historic architecture remaining intact.

On the corner of Ninth and Mitchell Streets, on the west side of a four-story building, the painter's choice of using white and black was wise, so as

not to blend into the tan-colored brick underneath. At first casual glance, the phrases "Big Ben" and "Self-Serv Shoes" remain clear and barely blemished. Underneath is the faint appearance of an arrow pointing to the right, explaining the bottom text: "Entrance Around Corner." However, if you look closely at the left of the sign beneath "Big Ben," there is evidence of faint red block print and what appears to be "John." This red print is also apparent in the upper right quadrant, albeit illegible.

The "John" refers to John's Bargain Store, which specialized in everything from housewares to clothing to appliances. It is presumed that after John's closed sometime in the 1960s, Big Ben's Shoes took residence and therefore painted directly over the original ad. Big Ben's sold men's, women's and children's shoes at bargain prices. It was one of the first stores in the area to offer the concept of "self-serve" shoes, contrary to the popular "full-service" fittings offered in the industry during this time.

ABOVE Big Ben Shoes on Mitchell Street sold men's, women's and children shoes. The entrance was around the corner from this sign.

WHITE EAGLE HOTEL

Also in the Mitchell Street neighborhood, on the northeast corner of South Eighth and West Maple Streets, we find the former White Eagle Hotel. This three-story brick vernacular commercial property was built in 1907. Simple and understated in design, this could be considered at best a moderate-level property and thus attracted a budget-minded clientele. Named after Poland's coat of arms, the "White Eagle" or "Orzel Bialy," the White Eagle Hotel claimed to be the first and only Polish-owned hotel in the city. Michael and Frances Wasilewski were listed as proprietors from 1920 through the late 1940s. Often frequented by locals, it was complete with a hall, billiards and a restaurant. "Gość w dom, Bóg w dom" (When the guest arrives, God arrives) was once the mission that guided the owners and staff and was displayed by the traditional Polish hospitality extended to all who entered.

"White Eagle Hotel 484" is still quite legible, despite the overall fading and blending into the brick façade. Outside of a few letters on the third line, possibly "BOS" followed by what appears as a "U" and a "K," deciphering the original content is difficult. The digits "484" were the original address, which was 484 Maple Street in the early 1920s. Therefore, the painting of this sign probably occurred in the 1920s or earlier.

The hotel was in operation until the 1980s and is believed to have been vacant for decades. One can only predict that this sorely dilapidated and neglected building will ultimately be demolished.

OPPOSITE White Eagle Hotel. A bit worse for wear. I'm pleasantly surprised this building on Eighth and Maple is still standing, given Milwaukee's enthusiasm for demolition.

GOLD MEDAL FLOUR

Sitting high above this former neighborhood grocery store in the Bayview neighborhood, we find a faded shadow-block print advertisement for Gold Medal Flour. This red-brick commercial vernacular building was built in 1910 with two separate storefront entrances on the lower level. There is a main entrance directly in the middle of the property, which was an unusual feature at the time. Beautiful oriel-style bay windows provide character to the second-story living quarters.

In 1866, Washburn-Crosby's Flour was formed and quickly became one of the most prominent brands in the industry. In 1880, when Washburn's Superlative Flour brand was awarded a gold medal at the First Millers International Exhibition, Gold Medal Flour was born. Celebrating its superior quality, a marketing slogan created in 1907 stated, "Eventually. Why Not Now?" Which is precisely what we see here. On the top line with a slightly angular script, the word "Eventually" can faintly still be seen. Within the circle, the words "Washburn-Crosby" have substantially faded into the underlying white brick below. The phrase "Why Not Now?" encompasses the lower edge of the ad. The advertising campaign ran the better part of fifty years, so it is difficult to determine exactly when this sign was painted.

Unfortunately, little can be found about the original shopkeeper. Based on the extensive fading and the type of font used, we can conclude that this sign was likely painted between 1920 and 1940. Today, the building is used for residential apartments.

OPPOSITE This Bay View apartment building dons an incredible faded brick painted ghost sign for Washburn Crosby's Gold Medal Flour, dating to 1900.

DISCOUNT LIQUOR MART

This prominent ad sits in the parking lot of Discount Liquor's former store at Forty-Fifth Street and West Forest Home Avenue. Based on the clues from the seven-digit phone number, the font and the Blatz slogan, the sign was likely painted sometime between 1965 and 1975. Discount Liquor opened in 1960 and enjoyed a booming operation until they closed in 1992.

On a black background in bold yellow font are the words "Discount Liquor Mart—We Deliver—Phone 545-2175—Open Daily 9–9 Sun 9–5," all of which are still clear and legible. The white lettering in the middle of the ad reminds patrons "Liquor Sold on Sunday," eliminating any confusion over Sunday liquor laws. In small black print in the lower left corner are three prominent brewery locations. What initially read, "Milwaukee, Peoria Heights, Los Angeles" has faded considerably. The sign is graced with the upper neck of a cool Blatz bottle and the Blatz slogan, "Smile, You've Got a Blatz Coming." This successful marketing campaign originated in the 1950s and was widely used well into the 1960s. The more precise slogan was "Smile, You've Got a Blatz *Beer* Coming." Blatz Brewing Company was one of the city's original three brewing giants, opening in 1851 and closing in 1959.

Valentin Blatz, a native of Bavaria, Germany, demonstrated a passion for the art and process of brewing. Valentin learned the craft from fellow Germans as an apprentice at his father's brewery in Bavaria, leading to further work at both the Born Brewery in Buffalo, New York, and John Braun's Cedar Brewery in Milwaukee. He formed his own brewery in Milwaukee in 1851. When Braun was killed in an accident in 1852, Valentin acquired his brewery and merged it with his own, forming City Brewery.

Over the next twenty years, Valentin grew his output from 800 barrels annually to 34,000 barrels in 1871. A fire destroyed much of the plant in 1872, which essentially paved the way for Valentin to update his new facility with the latest technology. By 1888, Blatz's City Brewery was producing more than 200,000 barrels a year. The Valentin Blatz Brewing Company incorporated in 1889 and would eventually become the city's third-largest and the nation's eighteenth-largest brewer. In 1894, Blatz passed away at the age of sixty-eight.

After surviving the Prohibition years, the brewery's name changed officially to Blatz Brewing Company. Pabst Brewing Company acquired Blatz from Schenley Industries. However, in 1959, the federal government, charging

that the acquisition violated Section 7 of the Clayton Act, prohibited the sale, resulting in the closing of Blatz Brewing. In 1960, Pabst purchased all of the remaining assets of Blatz, including rights to the label.

In 1969, the G. Heileman Brewing Company purchased the label from Pabst. Heileman was acquired by the Stroh Brewery Company in 1996, which sold it again to Pabst Brewing Company under the Miller Brewing Company in 1999.

Although the building is used only for storage today, the public can still relish this grand sign and relive the days when Blatz was a staple in the beer refrigerator.

ABOVE Discount Liquor's Blatz sign on Forty-Sixth Street and Forest Home Avenue. At the time, Blatz was the country's great light beer.

DRUG STORE

On the southwest corner of Forty-Third Street and Oklahoma Avenue, behind an alley lined with trash cans, we find a small, yet beautifully maintained, sign that reads, "Drug Store"—understated and leaving no indication as to the name of the pharmacy or any other details. The embellished font used here reflects a much earlier time, when this was painted, believed to be at or around 1960. Perhaps the font choice was intentional: the red-and-white-striped canopy resembles a picturesque storefront from an earlier decade, and the mortar and pestle represents the mixing and compounding commonly used by pharmacists before 1950.

John Shefchik was the owner and registered pharmacist here at the Jackson Park pharmacy from 1969 to 1995. Little is known about any prior occupants in this building, but there have been tales of a pharmacy before his ownership.

The sign reminds us of a bygone era: penny candy by the dozens; soda fountain counters offering bubbly drinks with various syrups and ice cream; and the neighborhood pharmacist, a highly respected member of the community who knew all of his customers personally and was a trusted friend to all.

OPPOSITE Jackson Park Pharmacy's alley signage from the building at the southwest corner of Forty-Third Street and West Oklahoma Avenue.

5

WALKER'S POINT

Situated just south of the Third Ward lies the Walker's Point neighborhood, founded by George H. Walker in 1835. Since its inception, the area has gone through much change, having been repurposed multiple times. It is one of the few neighborhoods in this book that was not inhabited by a dominant ethnic group, as the few that resided in the area primarily lived in the dual-purpose commercial/residential buildings.

Originally settled as a fur-trading post, the area transitioned into an industrial center in the latter half of the 1800s. Manufacturing in various sectors thrived throughout much of the twentieth century, where heavy machinery, clothing and textiles, food-processing plants and small retail businesses dominated the scene. During the final few decades of the century, as the trend toward offshore manufacturing grew, the area declined. Locally run businesses either closed or moved out resulting in decades of vacancies, abandonment and economic plight.

Revitalization efforts in the early 2000s brought new life to the area, with increased retail development, including a vibrant nightclub and restaurant scene. While the former warehouses and manufacturing plants have little utility today, they are being repurposed into trendy loft-style residential buildings and hotels.

There is growing concern that the faded ads in the area will be removed with this revitalization. Fortunately, the community maintains a strong focus on retaining and preserving the industrial influence that dominated the area for decades.

HEIL

Located on Ninth Street and National Avenue, at the addresses of 907–911 West National, the J.L. Burnham Block Building boasts a massive and well-preserved painted ad nearly two stories in height. This three-story, cream-city brick commercial Italianate structure was built in 1875 by Jonathan L. Burnham, a brickyard owner and real estate investor. Jonathan and his brother George moved from New York to Milwaukee in 1843. They quickly established themselves as the pioneers of Cream City brick. The building had an expansive top floor that was dedicated to events and affairs of all kinds, from weddings and balls to fundraisers and social meetings. German fraternal societies, labor unions and political assemblies gathered here for decades for strategic planning sessions and discussions aimed at solving the problems of the day. Many of the building's original features have remained intact, and cast-iron columns grace the front entrance.

Heil, a Milwaukee-based business founded in 1929, was the prime supplier of HVAC units to Sears. In 1957, Heil partnered with Sears before acquiring Quaker space heaters and the manufacturing plant from the parent company, Florence Stove Company. Based in Tennessee, Heil then left Milwaukee, moving the headquarters to the new Tennessee manufacturing plant. Heil-Quaker was eventually acquired by Inter-City Gas Corp in 1986, which, in turn, was acquired by Carrier in 1999.

The painted advertisement, listing only Heil, initially made me think that the sign must have been painted before the Heil-Quaker merger. However, the seven-digit telephone number indicates otherwise. It was more likely painted in the late 1960s or 1970s. The sign faces east and appears on the upper half of the building. Reliance Heating and Air Conditioning was a distributor and servicer of heating and cooling units. As the sign illustrates, Reliance and Heil must have established an exclusive partnership.

Part of this building, at 907 West National, is now utilized by local apparel company Milwaukee Home.

OPPOSITE A ghost sign that is reliant, cooling and warm. What else can you ask for?

THE GEORGE ZIEGLER COMPANY

Each immigrant group has shaped Milwaukee's rich history and culture. The flood of Germans in the mid-nineteenth century brought an incredible richness of flavor by way of food and drink traditions, recipes and processes from the homeland they desired to preserve and share for generations to come. While beer and sausage have long dominated the food and beverage industry in the city, chocolatiers and confectioners followed right behind. In 1845, George Ziegler immigrated to the United States from Harsheim Bavaria, Germany, as a teenager.

George moved to the city from the newly settled family farm in Columbus, Wisconsin. Here, he found mundane unskilled work in a general store and a shoemaking company before partnering with his two brothers-in-law in a candy-making business in 1861. By 1874, George had become the sole proprietor, and the company became the George Ziegler Company in 1887. His three sons joined; one son, Frank, would eventually become president in 1904.

Demand grew for the delectable chocolaty treats, forcing them into a larger factory, shown here, in 1907. Operations continued here until the business closed in 1972.

Ziegler Candy manufactured and sold a large variety of chocolates, candies and fruit and nut treats. But the biggest seller and claim to fame was the Giant Bar, or Ziegbar. The Ziegbar lives on. The public can still enjoy the famous Ziegbar, owned by fifth-generation Ziegler descendants. Half Nuts, a confectioner in West Allis, maintains the original candy molds.

The north-facing sign, roughly two stories in height, is well preserved despite the age. We can confidently place the sign's origin in the 1930s or 1940s based on the nickel candy bars sold during those decades. Due to the lack of a flat wall anywhere on the building, the ad is painted over an uneven surface facing north. The iconic Ziegler Giant Bar, or Ziegbar, is the focal point of the ad. The name "Ziegler's" hovers over the top of the bar, and the price, "5¢," is painted below.

Fortunately, we can still delight in the decadence of Ziegler Candy, despite the fading of the sign. The building has since been converted to residential apartments.

OPPOSITE In the 1960s, Ziegler's Candy handed out chocolate bars at local schools. The company was a Milwaukee institution for more than one hundred years.

INSELWOOD/STATE FAIR PARK/ PIONEER IMPROVEMENT COMPANY

A most unusual and surprising sight was exposed when a layer of siding was removed in 2018. This is the most bizarre sign in this collection, and we are left with so many questions about why it is here. Why was aluminum siding constructed directly over these signs? When did this happen? Was this done intentionally by the original contractors, leaving a time capsule to be unveiled in the distant future? While we may never know why these signs remained on the wall, dissecting each piece provides substantial clues to the period in which it was created.

Starting at the upper edge of the photo, we find two flattened cardboard boxes with green lettering: "Inselwood Grain-Tex" and "Exclusive Vapor Vent." Inselwood was one of several styles of insulated siding manufactured by a company called Inselbric. Incorporated in 1931, Inselbric produced an asphalt-based siding that provided the benefits of insulation and waterproofing, two desired features to protect homes from the harsh winter elements. This new technology was easy to install and maintain and could easily be customized to appear like real wood, stone or brick. This was graciously welcomed by owners of original wood-frame properties as a way to maintain a classic look without all of the upkeep. All of the Inselbric products remained popular until the 1960s, when aluminum siding grew in favor and continued to rise in popularity. These cardboard boxes were likely the very ones that held the content of the siding that was removed in 2018.

Directly below the Inselwood boxes is a poster that appears to be torn vertically in half. The left, in blue, reads "State Fair Park—Afternoon & Night—Monday and Tuesday—June." The word "Milwaukee" is obscured by a Pioneer Improvement Company poster. To the right in red lettering, "27 and 28" are the dates linked with "June" on the left. Those dates occurred in both 1938 and 1949. Based on what we know about Inselbric siding, either of those years can be feasibly considered as the time these ads were applied. However, the font and style lean toward the 1949 time frame.

In what appears to be a bumper sticker overlaying the State Fair Park sign, we see an ad for the Pioneer Improvement Company. This construction company, established in 1887, had been located at 3901 North Green Bay Avenue on the city's North Side. The bottom line reads "Manufacturers of

America's Broadest Line of Building Products," edged on both ends by the word "Flintkote" in a hexagonal shape.

The telephone is listed as "LOCUST 2-2213" in a format that was used in the 1940s and 1950s. This alone suggests that this ad was applied during or shortly after the summer of 1949.

ABOVE Old posted bills on the side of a building on Fifth Street in Walker's Point. The wall was exposed when construction workers removed a layer of siding. This is an amazing piece of Milwaukee history.

BADGER GLASS COMPANY

I recently spent time with David Magnasco, chef and proprietor of the Chef's Table restaurant, located at 500 South Third Street. He not only shared the fascinating history of the multiple areas of stenciling on the west-facing and north-side walls, but he was also a wealth of knowledge regarding the history of this building, dating back to 1913.

The sign itself was painted by Don Heyrman for the Badger Glass Company. The lettering is extremely faint and barely legible today. The sign appears to have fared much better on the right side of this photo, as this part of the image captures the west-facing view of the building. As the west side of the building has been shielded from the harsh winds off of Lake Michigan, I find this to be a credible explanation for the vast difference between the right and left sides. Observing the bottom-most left, the word "Glass" is still partially visible. However, the remainder of the print is a haphazard cluster of random letters. In contrast, the paint has faded more evenly on the right side. This makes it possible to read the words "Mirrors," "Plates" and "Glass." We can only guess what the remaining lettering at one time stated, and perhaps a different angle or lighting would reveal a few additional clues.

Directly above the door and obscured by the lamp, we can still see the digits "230." This three-digit number refers to the former address of 230 Hanover Street. In the early 1930s, to accommodate the growing population and the increase in privately owned cars, the city renamed and renumbered many of the streets in Milwaukee's downtown and adjacent neighborhoods. Hanover Street was in existence from the incorporation of Milwaukee through 1931 before being renamed Third Street, as it remains today. We can presume that "230" was painted on or around when Badger Glass opened in 1923 in conjunction with the rest of the signage. Badger Glass remained in operation until 1944.

In 1944, Eagle Knitting Mills joined with dozens of other textile factories in the area using this space not only as their production facility but also operating it as a warehouse and retail store. Around 1980, with production increasingly moving overseas, the Knit Pikker opened as a retail store for knitted goods.

It is so refreshing that, although several businesses have occupied the building over a time span of seventy-five years since the closure of Badger Glass, the lettering has remained unscathed and untouched.

The façade of this 1913 building is sprinkled with painted lettering dating back to the 1920s. Despite the fact that Badger Glass closed its doors in 1944, the signage has survived, reminding us of the services it provided.

EVERITT KNITTING COMPANY

Foremen hovering over workers, inspecting their work and barking orders to "work faster." Days were long. The work? Tedious. The pay? Atrocious and dismal. This was a common scene at the typical U.S. factory from the end of the nineteenth century and throughout most of the twentieth century.

Everitt Knitting Company was one of dozens of knitting mills in the Milwaukee area in the early 1900s. It manufactured everything from knitted caps, scarves and mittens to sewing belts, suspenders and epaulets. Textile production in Milwaukee at one time flourished, with dozens of knitting mills, heavily concentrated in the Third Ward and Walker's Point neighborhoods.

Dozens upon dozens of workers, predominantly women and children, lined up row after row, seated at tables, knitting. Hand-knitting would eventually be replaced by small manually operated mills and ultimately progressed into larger, automatic mills.

A more unusual sign, this one is painted directly on the glass door, as opposed to on the building itself. This Everitt Knitting door sits on the ground floor of the same building as the Louis Bass sign, discussed later in this chapter. The building was erected between 1890 and 1891 under the command of Captain Frederick Pabst.

Everitt Knitting was owned by Allen Davis Everitt. Records are inconclusive about whether he was the founder, but he was the owner and president until his death in 2006. It is also unclear if this sign was painted on a door leading to the factory or if these were corporate offices. Allen Everitt also owned a nearby building at 305 South Third Street, which was demolished in 2015. One of the last standing knitting mills in Milwaukee, Everitt Knitting closed in 2004 after ninety-four years in operation.

OPPOSITE Everitt Knitting, in Walker's Point, was one of many knitting mill factories that made designs for Garland, Sears and other companies.

HIGH-QUALITY...SHOES?

One of the oldest signs in this collection, it is also one of the most perplexing. A combination of nearly vanished print due to severe fading and difficult-to-find public records renders it utterly illegible. On the uppermost line, we can still read, "High Quality Of." The remainder of the sign is unreadable. Outside of a few letters, it is nearly impossible to string together a complete word. My first instinct was that this was another example of a sign painted over another. However, I am not convinced that is the case; instead, the incredibly faded print may be due to its age. It is possible that the only reason some remnants of writing remain is that the billboard was once placed directly over it, as evidenced by the metal frame. Public records have unfortunately not revealed much. The sign, outlined in what is now yellow, was likely painted in the late 1800s.

Frederick Gebelbauer built this two-story Cream City brick Italianate in 1886 at present-day 707 and 709 South Fifth Street. The upper levels provided housing, while the lower ground levels were established as a double storefront. There is a Frederick Gebelbauer listed in the 1888 City Directory at 305 Grove Street, which coincidentally became South Fifth Street following the 1931 street name conversion. The elder Frederick was a boot and shoe dealer, while the younger (listed as "junior") was a machinist. Somewhere among the faded lettering, the words "High Quality Of" must have at one time referred to shoes.

For approximately twenty years, between the 1930s and 1950s, Economy Sheet Metal was listed as the only occupant. Was this owned by the younger Frederick Gebelbauer? Unfortunately, we cannot find the answer to that question, although it is a distinct possibility.

While probable that several small-business owners had occupied these lower levels after the closing of Economy Sheet Metal, the building has been vacant for much of the last seventy years. Not surprising, the building appeared empty when I snapped the photograph.

OPPOSITE The Frederick Gabelbauer Building is a true mystery. Erected in 1886, it is listed in city records as housing a shoe- and bootmaker.

LOUIS BASS INC.

Louis Bass, a Jewish immigrant from Poland, owned a junk/salvage dealership and recycling yard here at South Third and West Florida Streets. This historic, five-story, 28,000-square-foot warehouse was built in 1890 for Captain Frederick Pabst. Otto Strack and C.L. Linde, two of the most prominent architects of the day, were hired to design this masterpiece. The result was a gorgeous Romanesque Revival structure, complete with arched windows and a grand arched entrance. At the top of the façade is a medallion graced with the letter "B" surrounded by sprigs of wheat, or "hops." Considering that this building was erected decades before Louis Bass assumed occupancy, it is a mystery what this letter signifies. One theory is that it is in reference to Jacob Best, founder of Pabst Brewery.

The building was initially rented by A.J. Lindemann & Hooverson, manufacturer of cooking appliances and water heaters, from their incorporation in 1892 through the early 1920s. After this time, Louis Bass moved in and remained at the warehouse for much of the twentieth century. As mentioned earlier in this book, Everitt Knitting also had space at this location.

The painted yellow banner on the uppermost floor appears restrained, yet it boldly proclaims the proud occupant below, "Louis Bass, Inc." The lettering was enclosed with a border on the top and bottom, although there has been significant fading on the top border, likely attributed to recent roof repairs. Here again, we find the letter "B" painted in a three-dimensional shadow font immediately before the name "Louis Bass." We can presume that the "B" was emblematic of the Bass name.

The building has been vacant for at least a decade, quite possibly longer. Since numerous warehouses in the area have been restored and repurposed into residential living and commercial space, one can only hope that this magnificent building holding both the Louis Bass and Everitt Knitting signs will be saved.

OPPOSITE Louis Bass Inc. was a successful junk dealership out of this historic building, which had been commissioned by one of the great Milwaukee beer barons, Captain Frederick Pabst.

FOX HEAD "400" BEER

Lying directly adjacent to and east of the Historic Mitchell Street neighborhood is Clock Tower Acres, separated by Interstate 94 and bordered by Greenfield Avenue to the north and both Becher Street and the Kinnickinnic River to the south.

This sign was quite a shock and a surprise to those removing the faux brick paneling from this 1890 commercial building in the summer of 2017.

The original sign is in pristine condition, as it was painted directly onto the original building paneling. It also appears that this ad was covered not too long after it was painted, having been subjected to minimal exposure from the elements. Partially covered here, the sign reads, "Fox Head '400' Beer." "Brewed with Waukesha Water" in red script completes the bottom of the sign, with the last word and several letters of "Waukesha" still obscured by the brick paneling. Without any hard evidence, we can tentatively conclude that the sign was likely painted in the early 1950s, based on the typescript, and it was covered shortly thereafter, as faux brick paneling gained popularity in the same decade.

Founded on the premise that Waukesha was known for its "high-quality water," Fox Head Brewing proudly touted the spring water as the basis of its beer being "healthy." The location was beyond perfect. With underground tunnels leading directly to the spring and with an extension to the railroad, one could not ask for a better location in terms of production and transport. The brewery was founded in 1893 and changed hands multiple times. Most notably, Fox Head Brewing was led by a female president in 1938, nearly unheard of at the time. Emilie Lindemann successfully led Fox Head through the most tumultuous times, surviving Prohibition, when most breweries collapsed. The Fox Head "400" label launched in 1936, shortly after Prohibition, and was one of the most successful and popular of all Fox Head products. A very sleek, polished and regal fox wearing a majestic grin was the symbol of Fox Head Brewing, further representing the quality beer being touted.

Its reputation was tarnished due to some unfortunate claims, true or not, linking Fox Head Beer to Chicago "mob" activity. Compounding the company's woes, ill-advised management, poor investment decisions and pervasive and declining quality forced Fox Head to close its doors in 1962.

The fate of the sign is unclear, but we can only hope that this unexpected unveiling of a piece of history will remain for all to enjoy for decades to come.

This Fox Head "400" Beer sign was uncovered after renovations next door at Transfer Pizzeria Café.

H.G. RAZALL MANUFACTURING COMPANY

Henry G. Razall was president of the H.G. Razall Manufacturing Company as early as the 1880s. The original location was not what we see here. The company was formerly located at 379 East Water, which became 1931 North Water Street after the 1931 street name conversions. Records show that this may have been the third location for the company. We do not know if it was the final location.

This three-story, Cream City brick, industrial loft located at both 1133 W Pierce Street and 710 South Twelfth Street was built in 1902. At the time of construction, it was considered both a loft and an expansive factory attached on the east elevation.

Razall owned the building, and the assumption is that a portion was leased out to William Zeige. I would presume that the sign was painted in the early 1900s, shortly after the building was erected. Enveloped in a white border, the sign reads:

THE H.G. RAZALL MANUFACTURING COMPANY
LITHOGRAPHERS AND PRINTERS
ANDRES AND ZEIGE ENG. CO.—GENERAL MACHINE SHOP.
[A faded arrow points left toward the main entrance.]

While not as apparent on the uppermost line of the sign, peering closely at the second line reveals remnants of faint writing underneath, indicating that a restoration once took place. This leads us to wonder if the original sign, which is assumed to have been painted in the early 1900s, was renovated with the arrival of Andres and Zeige, who leased space several decades later.

H.G. Razall Manufacturing specialized in the printing, production, binding and assembly of virtually all items required to record the written word. Black books, loose-leaf binders, leather-bound books, endless varieties of print, stationery and accounting ledgers were just a few of the items in which the company specialized. In 1890, it filed a bookbinding patent that they held for seventeen years. It must have been an incredible sight to see, with rows of printing presses and other general machinery used to assemble the vast amount of paper goods the company produced. In line with factories from this period, an abundance of manual labor was also required, necessitating the need for workers to be lined up at desks and tables throughout the facility to finish what the machines in those days could not.

Little is known about the Andres and Zeige Engineering Company, outside of the fact that it was a tool- and die-works manufacturer. William E. Zeige, born in 1898 in Menasha, Wisconsin, was president and general manager of Andres and Zeige Engineering. In December 1967, he died while driving to work at age sixty-nine. Based on his age, it is likely that the business did not open until the 1930s. This theory aligns with and supports the idea of an original and refurbished sign decades later.

OPPOSITE "Lithographers & Printers" is H.G. Razall Manufacturing. It printed books, stationery and other items. "Andres & Zeige Engine Co." was the name of a machine shop, also located here.

6

WEST SIDE

The signs in this section of Milwaukee are much newer overall than those in other chapters. Prior to the 1930s, much of this land was undeveloped and was composed primarily of farming communities and grain mills. Expansion into and settlement in the western areas grew exponentially during the post–World War II population and housing booms. Modest, three-bedroom Cape Cods and bungalows were constructed in the mid-1930s through 1960 for this predominantly middle-class, blue-collar community. While the West Side has been and still is today majority Caucasian, the area is becoming increasingly diverse.

Not to be confused with the Near West Side, which is the aggregate of seven neighborhoods to the immediate west of downtown, the images showcased in this chapter were largely captured on what is referred to as the Far West Side. This broad section extends north and south throughout the entire Milwaukee city limits and east to Fifty-First Street (although there is an exception or two here that lie just east of this border). Because of the extensive geography, a distinct culture here is difficult to define and describe.

DODGE CITY

"Get out of Dodge!" This is a direct reference to Dodge City, Kansas, a busy cattle town in the late nineteenth century. Most people remember it as the line made famous in the popular Western television series *Gunsmoke* (1952–75). Quite simply, the phrase urges one to leave a dangerous situation—urgently.

In the sign's wise play on words, the word *Dodge* is also a reference to AMC Dodge vehicles. Dodge City is an auto dealership located in the heavily commercialized and congested thoroughfare at Twenty-Seventh Street and Layton Avenue. This intersection separates the city of Milwaukee from the city of Greenfield, also within Milwaukee County.

The whimsical cowboy hat, tattered with holes and with arrows remaining, is immensely recognizable in the Milwaukee community. Owned by the Schlossman Auto Group, the Dodge City auto dealership was extremely successful in the 1970s and beyond at this location. It has since relocated to Brookfield. Schlossman's Honda City and Subaru City now bear the same tattered and arrow-riddled hat logo.

OPPOSITE Dodge City. "We're the good guys in the white hats." This is one of the last remnants from the car dealer on Layton Avenue.

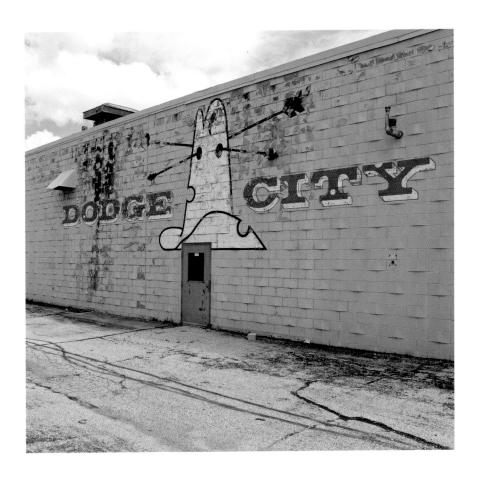

MARQUARDT'S PHARMACY

Located a few blocks from the Wheaton Franciscan–St. Joseph's Campus, the former Marquardt's Pharmacy sits on the northwest corner of Fifty-Third and West Burleigh. Eleanore and Oswald Marquardt owned and operated the pharmacy beginning sometime in the late 1920s until 1956. It eventually became Burleigh Serv-U Pharmacy, which closed in 2010. Today, a mini-market operates on the main level.

This colorful beauty sits above the parking lot on the west side of the building and reads:

[Green box] MARQUARDTS PHARMACY.
[In a smaller, italicized print between both words, we can faintly see the word "Prescription."]
[Yellow/brown box] WE DELIVER—CALL HL5-9664.
[Red box] SEALTEST ICE CREAM
[Black box] WILLIAMS BEAUTY STUDIO
[Black box, lower left] NORTHERN SIGN COMPANY
[Bottom box] ENTRANCE AROUND CORNER

This sign provides us with insightful clues about when it was painted, with the phone number providing the most clarity. The phone number was HI, the abbreviation for "Hilltop." This alone allows us to conclude that the sign was painted in the 1950s or 1960s. While we know that the pharmacy was on the lower level, was Williams Beauty Studio on the upper? While Eleanore and Oswald resided in the living quarters above the store, it is entirely feasible that the beauty studio rented out a room or two upstairs in which to take clients. Or, was this sign leading to a nearby building? No information can be found to support either theory, so we will have to be satisfied with what we know to be facts and leave the rest to imagination.

OPPOSITE This Marquardt's Pharmacy sign in Sherman Park is in great condition, as it was blocked by another building for quite some time after the building was demolished.

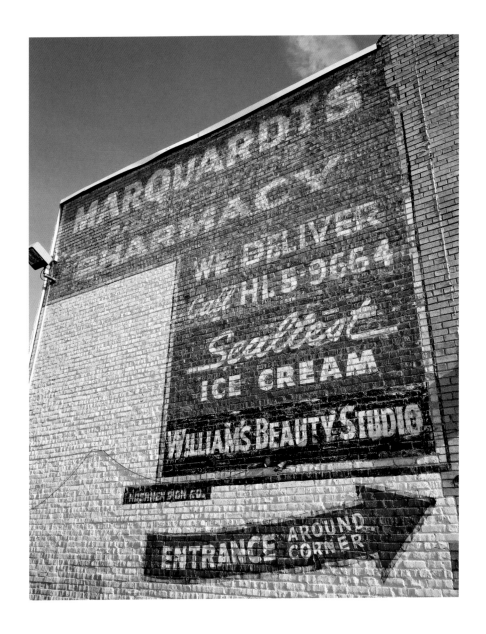

MILWAUKEE NUT COMPANY

Traveling through the quaint Martin Drive neighborhood, this sign is easy to miss and difficult to spot. This cute little sign is tucked away on what would be the side of Forty-Third Street. It is only visible in the colder months, as it is obscured by trees and bushes when in bloom. It sits above the sidewalk at eye level for the average adult. It may be four feet in length and two feet in width at best. With a fading yellow background, we find a profile of a squirrel holding what is perhaps a tool in the manual nut-roasting process. The writing is scuffed in a few places but still very much legible: "Milwaukee—Nut Co.—Food Distributors."

A small, quaint and close-knit diverse community on the city's West Side nestled between Washington Park and the Miller Valley district. Here you will find mature trees, midcentury homes and one-way streets. The building, Art Deco in design, directly faces Washington Park. There are no windows in the front of the building. However, this sign does appear to be painted on glass—one of the few side windows on the building.

The Milwaukee Nut Company was in operation for approximately sixty years. Its specialties lay in a wide variety of nuts, candies and dried fruit, all of which were delectably prepared on the premises and distributed to a wide range of businesses and consumers. Today, the building is utilized as a 3,150-square-foot warehouse storage facility.

OPPOSITE Milwaukee Nut sign, located on the corner of Forty-Third and Vliet in Washington Park. It was a Nut Company Food Distributor.

JOHNSON'S PARK

Aaahhh! The memories! I have such fond childhood memories of Johnson's Park, as do thousands of other Milwaukeeans who grew up in the 1970s and 1980s. The sign itself is dull and seemingly insignificant. However, ask any Milwaukee native over the age of forty, and you will see lips turn upward into a smile and perhaps even spot a glisten in their eye.

The contagious laughter of children, the roar of go-karts and the smack of a baseball. The indistinguishable sounds erupting from the game room. You can still hear the sounds ever so faintly when standing at 7350 North Seventy-Sixth Street. This sign is the last remaining remnant of Johnson's Park, which operated from the 1970s through the mid-1990s.

Located on the city's Northwest Side at Seventy-Sixth and Good Hope, Johnson's Park provided endless entertainment with go-karts, mini-golf, a video arcade and a giant slide. With two eighteen-hole golf ranges and major-league-level batting cages, this was a place for families and teenagers alike. The park peaked in popularity in the 1980s, when I was a child.

The fantasyland theme of the golf course was whimsical and light. The oversized figures were brought to life through psychedelic patterns and bright, vibrant colors. It was a strange blend of nursery rhyme characters and Alice in Wonderland–like eclecticism. There were human-sized fish, a pumpkin stagecoach and a wise owl. An ostrich caused distractions by bobbing its head over the hole. There was Moby Dick, Wooly Worm, the Old Lady who lived in a Shoe and a Flying Saucer, to name a few. An igloo ended the adventure unless you earned a free game by putting a hole-in-one!

Everything was fun and light, except for one menacing character: the Tyrannosaurus Rex. He stood more than sixteen feet tall and dared anyone to putt the golf ball past him. T-Rex leaned on a bone, perhaps a femur left over from a victim, which he seemed to use as a cane (or weapon). With the other arm, he repeatedly raised and lowered an obstacle, requiring perfect timing to putt the ball past him.

Abandoned in 2000, the busted windmill and decaying T-Rex sat on the property for decades. I am not sure what happened to the windmill, but the mighty T-Rex was the last standing character. He was ultimately saved, auctioned off for a bargain price of eleven dollars. He now has a permanent home and is being restored. While the site of Johnson's Park remains desolate, empty and vacant, the memories will live on forever.

ABOVE This sign is the last remnant from Johnson's Park & Mini Golf. Many people spent hours and dollars here. There was an arcade, go-karts and batting cages.

ROOB PHOTOGRAPHY

This sign is a peculiar mural that is less an advertisement and more of a tribute. Painted in 1972 on a dark charcoal background is the caricatured representation of the Roob family. Walter Roob was an extremely popular and successful family photographer who captured the most important moments of the lives of millions in the city over six decades.

Clients of Roob recall his professionalism and ability to elicit emotion. Children made their annual pilgrimage to the Roob Studios wearing their Sunday best, to be snapped with the "live" Easter lamb. Still others returned year after year. From capturing the toothless grin of a kindergartener to the smile of a blossoming teenager ready to conquer the world at high school graduation, Roob was entrusted to forever preserve these memories.

The mural captures three, possibly four, generations of the Roob family. The sign itself is in the rear of the building facing the parking lot. Roob himself is whimsically characterized on the far left edge of the mural, pictured where he loved to spend his time—behind the camera. Roob, depicted with an old-style camera sitting on a tripod, is covered by a shroud as he peers into the lens.

The mural emanates love, happiness and the togetherness of family. Walter's passion for photography is demonstrated here and passed on through the generations. Although Walter has since retired, Roob Photography lives on through Jonathan Roob, who carries on the Roob name and the love for photography.

The Roob signature on the lower corner and the back of photos still graces the mantels in homes across Milwaukee spanning six decades. Roob, however, did not leave his name on this painted mural.

OPPOSITE TOP Roob Photography Mural 1. The mural is still on the side of the former studio on Seventy-Eighth Street and Appleton Avenue.

OPPOSITE BOTTOM Roob Photography Mural 2. In the 1970s, most Milwaukee families had their photos taken here. Walter Roob was a household name in Milwaukee.

SCARDINA BAKERY

The third and final local Italian bakery/deli in this book, Scardina Bakery was enjoyed by residents living in this West Allis neighborhood. A photo discovered from 2014 shows clear, bright and vivid red script with distinct artwork on both sides. What is perplexing is that, once again, we find that one of the newer signs in this collection is extremely faded and decayed, short of the average expectancy with these ads. In this case, with the banning of lead paint in 1978 and apparent rapid deterioration, I suspect that a non-lead-based paint was used.

Founded in 1971, this Scardina's location is permanently closed. The name "Scardina" is faded on the top line. The second line reads, "Italian French Bread Rolls Cookies Cannoli." Interestingly enough, none of these words are painted; instead, either a raised metal or an acrylic lettering was used.

We have seen dozens of examples in this book alone in which ghost signs have remained relatively intact for eighty years or more. Why is the painting on the top line so drastically faded? Was an attempt made to deliberately remove the name? Why has the lettering on the second line not yet been removed? Also nearly indistinguishable, to the left of "Scardina," is a drawing representing the country of Italy. It is barely recognizable. The artwork to the right was at one time a portrait, presumably of the owner. This sign, unfortunately, inspires more questions than answers.

OPPOSITE Scardina Bakery in West Allis was a place where locals could satisfy their cravings for ham and rolls and other treats.

ROUNDY'S FOODS

This is another example of a ghost sign that is not an advertisement at all but has left a mark and historic preservation in the mind of Milwaukeeans. This now-vacant thirty-acre parcel on the city's far Northwest Side is the former warehouse and distribution center for Roundy's Foods.

Founded in 1872 in Milwaukee, Roundy's initially operated as Smith, Roundy and Company by way of the partnership among William E. Smith, Judson Roundy and Sidney Hauxhurst. Over the next four decades, ownership changed hands several times, but the Roundy's name was always retained. Finally, in 1922, the food chain settled on simply "Roundy's."

ABOVE Roundy's Foods Warehouse sign is a remnant of the once-sprawling distribution complex on Burleigh in Wauwatosa.

OPPOSITE The Roundy's Foods Warehouse sign stands on top the former distribution center like some sort of postindustrial art installation. The letters will be used for an art installation or branding piece in the next phase to the property.

GROCERY
Receiving
ONLY

USE CITIZEN BAND RADIO
Channel #
FOR INSTRUCTIONS

Roundy's was one of the leading grocers in the Midwest, with over 150 stores, and it was the top chain in the Milwaukee area. In 2015, Roundy's was acquired by Kroger Company, based in Cincinnati. Fortunately, this acquisition allowed for the continuation of the Roundy's Brand Products and operation of its stores (Copps, Metro Market, Pick 'n Save and Mariano's) without disruption.

The painted sign is virtually flawless. Several key characteristics point to when the application of this sign occurred. The sign leaves no hint of having undergone a restoration, yet outside of some chipping on the white background, it seems as though it was freshly painted not long ago. The font selected and the mention of CB radio (short for "citizens band radio") lead us to believe that this was painted in the mid-1970s. With the lead-paint ban occurring in 1978, we can almost assume that, considering the resiliency of this sign, lead-based paint had been used. CB radio, starting in the late 1950s, surged in popularity in the 1970s and into the 1980s. With little to no utility today, CB radio communications have been replaced with cellular and internet services.

The following sign sits on top of the building in the form of acrylic or plastic-based lettering. This may have been lighted at one time, but it is difficult to ascertain this from a distance.

These signs will eventually meet their fate. They are located on vacant land that once bustled with loaded semi-trucks transporting goods among suppliers, warehouses and the more than one hundred Roundy's locations. The site now sits quiet and empty. The land will undoubtedly be sold and occupied in the future, which will lead to the signs' ultimate demise.

7

WESTERN SUBURBS, TOWNS AND VILLAGES

We now extend our journey to the westward neighbors of Milwaukee that were—and still are—an integral part of the landscape of the city. Most of these towns lie within forty miles of downtown Milwaukee. They were important centers of activity, connected by waterways and railroads in the early days. These were both quaint resort towns and farming communities.

A plank road was constructed in 1850 connecting several of the featured towns in this chapter—including Pewaukee, Waukesha, Oconomowoc and Watertown—to Milwaukee.

Waukesha, once known as "Prairieville," was settled by Morris Cutler in 1834. The first settlers were the Native American tribes comprising the Potawatomi, Menomonee and Ho-Chunk. Agriculture in the form of corn, berries and varieties of pumpkin and squash was the mainstay. Game such as deer and wild turkey were hunted. As the English, Scottish, Irish and German settlers slowly displaced all three tribes, grain, lumber and flour mills were established to complement the agriculture already in place. Waukesha, like several of the other towns to be discussed here, was once considered a "resort town" due to the abundance of pristine lakes and rivers, including the Fox River. Today, Waukesha bears little resemblance to what it once was, having grown immensely into essentially an extension of the city of Milwaukee. Waukesha celebrates both a booming economy supported by industry and corporate offices and a healthy housing market.

FRIEDMAN'S CLOTHES SHOP (WAUKESHA)

When this grand sign was painted, it must have been applied with great conviction, as if it was never intended to be removed. Even the colors used are some of the most vibrant and intense in this collection. Friedman's Mens Wear had its home at 250 West Main Street in Waukesha for nearly fifty years.

In 1934, Samuel and Mabel Friedman opened Friedman's Clothes Shop. Mr. Friedman owned several properties in downtown Waukesha, including several hotels, one of which was converted in the early 1950s to the Friedman Apartments.

The sign was erected in the 1940s or 1950s. Painted in a vibrant hue of red, it reads, "Friedman's Mens Wear—Home of National Brands." Our eyes, however, are drawn to the advertisement for Oshkosh B'Gosh, "The World's Best Overall," which appears above Friedman's name. Friedman may have been an exclusive provider of the Wisconsin brand, which specialized in workers' clothing, including its famous "painter pants" and "bibbed overalls."

As Sam neared retirement, Friedman's Mens Wear closed its doors in 1967. What I find curious, interestingly enough, is that since its closing, more than a dozen establishments have resided here. Outside of several short vacancy periods, the majority of businesses have not been able to keep afloat for more than two years. I wonder why this is so.

OPPOSITE This Oshkosh B'Gosh sign in Waukesha, Wisconsin, was restored by Bill Taylor. He donated his time, materials and talent to bring it back to life.

LYNNDALE FARMS RACEWAY (PEWAUKEE)

This is a spectacular find. Imagine this scenario: You drive past an old building or, in this instance, a barn, day after day. Week after week. Month after month. You glance over and see nothing particular of note except a decades-old barn with fading and chipping paint. Then, one day, you have to take a second look as you notice an advertisement taking over the once-barren wall. The strange thing is that the ad was not newly painted. It was unearthed after decades of hiding.

In 2017, this experience happened to countless residents and passersby in this Pewaukee neighborhood. This decades-old sign, hidden behind a coat of chipped white paint on the side of a barn, advertised the long-defunct Lynndale Farms Raceway. The sign had been covered with a basic white paint years later. On removing the layer of paint, this beauty was revealed. After the racetrack closed in 1967, the owner, Jerry Hirsch, subdivided the land into residential lots; portions of the track remain today.

This impressive sign extends to the entire wood-planked side of the barn. In all capital letters on the top line to the left is "Lynndale"; the line below, in lowercase, reads, "road racing course." The final word is still heavily obscured by white paint, but several letters are still somewhat visible.

To the right, "Sinclair Dinosaur. Sinclair Dino Supreme" is separated from the writing above by the cartoonish image of the Sinclair dinosaur.

The Lynndale Farms Road Racing Course opened in 1963 and offered sports-car races, motorcycle races and auto shows. Unbelievable as it may sound, the small town of Pewaukee was home to one of the top-ten racetracks in the nation. However, natives know too well how the unpredictable Wisconsin weather tends to hinder outdoor activities, regardless of the season. The combination of frequently canceled races and the growing complaints about the noise voiced by neighbors forced the raceway to close in 1967.

The fate of the sign is unknown, but with the outpouring of public support and fascination, the hopes are that the remainder of the white paint will be removed and full restoration pursued.

OPPOSITE Former Lynndale Farms Raceway ghost sign in Pewaukee. In early 2018, the sign was uncovered.

AMERICAN DRY CLEANERS AND LAUNDERERS (BUTLER)

It is officially registered within the town of Butler, just on the outskirts of Milwaukee County. American Dry Cleaners and Launderers at 4701 North 124th Street sadly closed its doors in 2018 after ninety-two years in business. In the earlier decades of the 1920s, 1930s and 1940s, it was primarily used as a railroad laundromat, as it was built near the major railways.

Displaying the unique architecture found throughout this collection, this eclectic midcentury modern is a one-story commercial building boasting floor-to-ceiling windows covering the entire storefront. The main building was constructed with Lannon stone, while the cornered extensions were brick composite and cement block. The circular driveway doubles as a drive-through under a large carport in the front of the building.

The sign, painted over cement block, was applied on a wall facing a parking lot. While the whitewashed base is peeling in a few areas, the painted script in dark blue is still intact and legible. Without further clues—and given the establishment's lifespan of more than ninety years—it is nearly impossible to conclude when and who applied this advertisement.

OPPOSITE Midcentury Modern, 1950s architecture is illustrated here. American Dry Cleaners on 124th between Hampton and Capitol Drive offered rug cleaning.

THE SCHLITZ HOTEL (OCONOMOWOC)

Oconomowoc, thirty-five miles directly west of Milwaukee, was once considered a "playground for the wealthy" due to its pristine and lush landscapes. Oconomowoc entertained six U.S. presidents in the late nineteenth century, as they came to enjoy the splendor and relaxation the quaint town provided. Each of them, of course, were guests of the luxury hotels and properties in operation at that time.

The Schlitz Hotel was built in August 1901 on the corner of Main and Collins Streets. Convenient to the primary mode of transportation of the day, it was built directly across from the train depot. This two-story, Cream City brick hotel, similar to the bed-and-breakfast inns of today, comprised a public dining room and twelve guest rooms. Further entertainment was provided to residents and hotel guests by the Palm Garden and Tap Room. It was considered a luxury hotel; each floor had a bathroom and steam heat. All the comforts of home were said to be provided.

Like many historic homes and hotels, there are stories hidden in the walls. Here at the Schlitz Hotel, if those walls could talk, we could undoubtedly hear Jim Doherty, bartender and operator of the Palm Garden and Tap Room, muttering a few choice words over what happened one disastrous evening in 1936, which happened to be Christmas Eve. The phrase "Cocktail Hour"—"Happy Hour" as we know it today—was used much as it is today, that is, to drum up business in the late afternoon and early evening hours. In his brilliance, he came up with an idea that, as it turns out, was ill-conceived and short-sighted. He advertised a "cocktail hour" special whereby every patron would get a free drink of the one previously purchased each time the Hiawatha train passed by. Jim was elated as the crowds of men gathered and flocked to the bar to partake in this brilliant marketing idea. Jim looked out at the jovial group, proud of his success. Then, the Hiawatha train passed, sounded its horn, everyone cheered in jubilation and Jim promptly served each and every one of them their free drink. Now, you can just imagine what happened next. The guests knew much more than poor Jim did and remained at the bar until the train passed again. They cheered and raised their glasses, and Jim had no choice but to honor his special. As he reluctantly poured the next round, the cash register rang up empty. The guests knew that the Hiawatha was not yet finished for the evening. The train traveled through town again that night—seven more times.

The sign, faded beyond recognition, is painted at the rear of the building. Faintly visible are the partial words that originally spelled "Hotel Schlitz" surrounding the globe encased with a sash, the emblem of Schlitz that we saw earlier in this collection. Several attributes of the sign seem odd. The red background appears to shape the lettering and globe, much like a stencil. In other words, the lettering and globe do not look as if they were ever painted, as was common practice. Instead, both are composed only of the original bricks, whereas the red background simply surrounds the formations. Also, the chimney lying near the middle of the ad does not appear to have any paint whatsoever. Was it neglected from the beginning, or has the paint simply faded completely? This sign needs a significant restoration—soon. At this time, there have been no published efforts to do so.

OPPOSITE The Schlitz Hotel building looks the same today as it did more than one hundred years ago. The establishment served the beer that made Milwaukee famous.

WRIGLEY'S SPEARMINT (WATERTOWN)

Sometimes, the subject of the ad is all that is needed to narrow down the dates of painting. On the west side of this building, partially hidden by an adjacent building, is one of the most intriguing ghost signs in Watertown.

The slogan "Sealed in Its Purity Package" was used by Wrigley's Spearmint from approximately 1914 to 1925. The spear-bodied elf character, William Wrigley, was introduced into this advertising campaign in 1914. Spearmint, an herb with pointy leaves, is represented by the sharp point on the elf's head. William Wrigley was sometimes referred to as a "spearman." "Purity Package" refers to the thin, individually wrapped foil gum packages—foil seals in the freshness.

This ghost sign dates to 1922. At one time, this must have been a vibrantly colored sign. The only section that remains distinctly visible is the center, with the image of the gum package. The upper two lines in yellow are smeared and bleeding, nearly illegible. We know only from the historical slogan that it reads, "Sealed in Its Purity Package." The whimsical "spearman" is smiling to the left and above the Wrigley gum package. Beneath the gum in a black-shaded section, "The Flavor Lasts" is still distinguishable. The remainder of writing is unrecognizable, and it is impossible to guess what may have been there at one time.

This adjoined property, located at 713 to 715 West Main Street, was built in 1900. Between the years of 1910 and 1924, the Hotel Restaurant and Woelffer's Place, a saloon, occupied both units. Records are unclear about what the property was used for after 1924. In the 1950s, Miller Auto Replacement Parts occupied the building and remained in business through the 1980s. In 2013, Morgan's Roadhouse Bar and Grill enjoyed a short stint here before turning it over to the current occupants, Cherry Bomb Beer and Burgers.

OPPOSITE Wrigley's Spearmint Gum. The slogan "Sealed in its purity package" was used by Wrigley's Spearmint from approximately 1914 to 1922. Located in Waterford, the sign dates to 1922.

GETTELMAN'S BREWERY (WAUKESHA)

This is a beautiful ghost sign for Gettelman Beer, painted on a hotel/rooming house wall in downtown Waukesha. Missing only approximately a two-foot portion at the top of the sign, it has remained pristine despite the apparently advanced age.

As Gettelman's was purchased in 1961 by Miller Brewing Company, we can presume that this was painted in the 1950s. The original "$1,000" process beer was accentuated with gold-labeled bottles and completely golden cans. Adam Gettelman launched the famous "$1,000 Natural Process" campaign in 1891. The campaign promised a monetary prize of $1,000 to anyone able to prove that Gettelman's premium beer was brewed with anything but pure malt, hops and water. Many tried, but no one was ever able to prove otherwise, and the money forever remained unclaimed.

The sign was commissioned by Derse Advertising, noted at the lower left underneath the painted ad. In 1948, James F. Derse founded the Derse Company as a sign-painting business in the back of his mother's Milwaukee garage. The chalice bears the Gettelman name, and the banner below reads, "Milwaukee Beer." The images are distinct and still, yet despite fading, they still bear bold colors. The Wisconsin Hotel operated for decades under this roof, making it highly probable that there was an area dedicated on the main level that served as a bar or a taproom. Based on the information discovered, it is safe to assume that this gem was painted in the 1950s.

Today, the Wisconsin House, providing weekly and short-term rental options, occupies all of this 1910 building.

OPPOSITE Gettelman Brewing Company almost made Milwaukee famous. This sign is located in downtown Waukesha on Main Street.

8

FADED ROAD SIGNS

Our final chapter displays a fine collection of metal, neon and lighted signs.

Composed of steel in the early days before transitioning to aluminum, metal road signs came into use across the United States in the mid- to late 1920s. Of note, Wisconsin was the first state in the union to mandate road signs, in 1918, to impose sense out of the disorderly and uncontrolled traffic. However, it was not until 1927 that a national manual was published mandating standardization of signs to avoid confusion across state lines. For example, the octagon forever became known as the stop sign; a round sign was only to be used for railroad crossings; and the rectangle was to be used for warnings and as precautionary informational signs. Over the years, the colors have been changed and the paint improved several times to minimize light scattering caused by rain droplets and to increase overall reflectiveness.

The neon lamp was developed by a French inventor, Georges Claude, in 1902. The first two signs sold to the United States were purchased by a Packard car dealership in Los Angeles for a whopping $24,000. The public was in awe of these magnificent signs. (Neon was nicknamed "liquid fire.") They certainly had pizazz and allure over the traditional painted sign, which could not be seen in the evening.

Neon and lighted signs increased in prevalence in the 1930s. While the lighted sign was either a "light box" that was internally illuminated by a standard light source or one with multiple exterior bulbs, the neon sign was constructed with gas-filled tubing. Some were simple, but most were extravagant, with curved and swirled tubing assuming shapes never before seen with lighting. With variations of flashing, dimming and chasing lights and a wide array of bold and bright colors, they were a pure spectacle. The streets of downtowns in major cities and even in small towns across the United States were decorated with these shimmering and flashing lighted signs. It was just as common to find a roadside diner on a desolate highway decorated with these grand spectacles as it was to find bold, flashy neon signs lining the casinos on the streets of Las Vegas. From theaters to gas stations, from restaurants to cocktail lounges, neon and metal signs were attention-grabbing and representative of midcentury Americana.

The other benefit of this new trend in signage is that these did not have the permanence of painted ads plastered on a building itself. They also offered flexibility in placement, as they could be erected close to a road, in a parking lot or anywhere else desired to gain maximum visibility. There was no longer a need to hire a sign painter. The most significant issues posed by these metal signs, of course, is that they become rusted and difficult to restore, in contrast to fading ads, which can be repainted. These rusting displays, with broken tubes and lights and hanging wires, are seen by some as an eyesore. Some signs cling to life by hanging by a thin strand of rusted metal. However, a new era dawned in the late-1960s as neon signs, which had been so popular for decades, were now seen as unnecessarily boastful and tacky. Production of new signs steeply declined. Likewise, repair and restoration of these decaying signs nearly came to a halt.

Most signs here represent a defunct business, much like those in the previous seven chapters, and each has a story to share. After the business closed, the sign remained—neglected and a far cry from the flashing lights and vibrancy they once proudly displayed.

ART'S PUPPY LODGE

On a rural stretch of road on Milwaukee's Northwest Side, tucked away among the trees and foliage, this little gem peeks out, hoping not to be ignored. Amid overgrown shrubbery and brush, it lies at 7311 Granville Road.

The Art's Puppy Lodge sign was tucked away on the Northwest Side. The grounds are now host to a pet cemetery, and the sign was recently removed for unknown reasons.

Underneath the playfully hanging tongue of a mischievous dog lies the advertisement for "Art's Puppy Lodge—Kennels—Boarding." Neon tubing outlines each alphanumeric piece. It doesn't appear the dog itself has any neon tubes, but it may have been backlit with one or more bulbs.

Now it is the location of Pet Lawn, a pet cremation service and cemetery. As you approach the property via the gravel entrance, you can still see the abandoned chain-link-fenced cages where the dogs had been granted their outdoor play time. The place looks sadly quiet and serene today, but you can still sense the liveliness and joy that presided here at one time, when thousands of dogs mingled and made new friends, anxiously awaiting the return of their owners.

In 1946, Adam Feist invested in an 8-acre parcel sold to him by the Evert family, owners of 320 acres of land. Two short years later, Adam sold his portion to Arthur Gueltzow, who established Art's Puppy Lodge. A home away from home for various pets, its predominant guests were canines.

Ownership changed hands several times, and Richard "Dick" Bernier eventually purchased the property in 1967. He proceeded to establish a crematorium on the site, which was a separate business entity, Pet Lawn. Dick passed away in 2010, and the land was eventually sold to Dr. Kristen Rowe, DVM, in 2013. The following year, the Memorial Garden was established to honor all those who had once enjoyed the grounds. When Kristen passed away in 2016, her brother Brennan continued to operate the business.

More than ten thousand pets are buried here, including cats, dogs, reptiles, guinea pigs, horses, birds and rabbits. Three people have also chosen this as their final resting place. Essentially, every breed or species that was once a beloved member of the family has been laid to rest here. Sadly, the sign was removed in 2018.

ERNIE VON SCHLEDORN (MENOMONEE FALLS)

"Who do ya know wants to buy or lease a car or truck?" asked a man with a glimmer in his eye and a melodic voice that made you feel as if you were conversing with a longtime friend. This question was posed by Ernie von Schledorn in his distinctive, thick German accent. His kind request for customer referrals sang from his radio and television commercials into the living rooms of millions of people in southeastern Wisconsin throughout the decades. The slogan never changed. Every commercial ended with a trio of female singers with the lyrics, "Ernie von Schledorn…Main Street in Menomonee Falls." It was one of the most memorable jingles from my childhood, and I can still hear it as perfectly today as if it had just sounded from my television.

Ernie von Schledorn was a household name in the Milwaukee area. By trade, he was an auto dealer specializing in GMCs, Buicks and Volkswagens. Ernie, a native of West Germany, immigrated to the United States and, in 1952, with fourteen dollars in his pocket, hitchhiked from the East Coast until he was dropped off in Milwaukee. After working a variety of odd jobs, Ernie landed a position with Edwards Motor Company in 1955. Within two short years, he became the number one sales representative in the United States. Jovial, friendly and dynamic, he drew others with his bubbly personality and professionalism. In 1959, Ernie opened his own dealership on the city's Northeast Side at 400 East Capitol Drive. Achieving phenomenal success, in 1965, he established this second location in Menomonee Falls, specializing in Pontiacs and Buicks. He opened several dealerships in the area, but this location was deemed the "flagship."

Needing no further description, the sign here reads "EVS," the well-known abbreviation for "Ernie von Schledorn." Pointing toward the showroom and car lot, this sign may have been the original from the 1960s. The two painted posts holding up the former lighted box show excessive peeling and are begging for a paint job. Damage is evident on the lower part of the sign over the word "Cars." The lot where this relic resides is now abandoned and has been purchased for redevelopment into a corporate campus.

Ernie enjoyed a sixty-year career during which he remained a visible business and community leader, until his death at the age of eighty-eight in November 2014. Although he is no longer physically with us, his contagious spirit will live on forever in the hearts of Milwaukeeans.

OPPOSITE "Who do ya know wants to buy or lease a car or truck?" was car salesman Ernie von Schledorn's tagline at the end of his commercials.

DISCOUNT LIQUOR

This sign is soon to be destined for the trash. Located at Forty-Fifth Street and West Forest Home Avenue, this is the same Discount Liquor sign discussed earlier. Whereas the painted ad lies on the rear wall, this sign was planted in the front parking lot, beckoning drivers to follow the arrow for a deal.

Badly battered and tarnished, replete with missing bulbs and lettering, this formerly flashy sign must have been a sight to see in its prime. It once glowed with bright red lights; they may have been chasing lights, starting at the top and ending at the arrow pointing toward the entrance. The lower rectangular piece of the sign most likely had the same white fitting as each letter but may have been removable, providing the flexibility to advertise specials.

In cursive script, the word "Discount" had once been lit with white neon tubing. There are vertically displayed letters that compose the word "Liquor." Each letter sits on its own white plastic light covering that was at one time shone white and red lighting. The rectangular section on the bottom of the sign presumably had removable lettering for advertising specials and posting other essential messages. Based on the condition, we can probably assume that this was erected in the 1960s, much like the Blatz sign painted on the rear wall shown earlier in this book.

OPPOSITE Discount Liquor's former store stood on Forty-Fifth and West Forest Home Avenue until 1992. The sign still stands as a reminder.

NO PARKING

Near 500 North Mitchell Boulevard, there is a low brick barrier wall adjacent to the sidewalk. This is the same bridge that crosses over Interstate 94. Hundreds of baseball fans park in this vicinity to avoid parking fees or appreciate more convenience—or a combination of both. The downside was that there was a high risk for ticketing and towing, making one wonder why anyone would make this decision.

This sign, although badly rusted, is still legible. Having experienced many winters submerged in snow, this comes as no surprise to me. Adhered to a low concrete barrier, it is so low to the ground and obscure that I can only imagine how many "missed" the sign and met the costly fate of ticketing—or, worse yet, were unable to locate their car to discover it was in the City of Milwaukee Tow Lot.

The sign reads: "No Parking During Stadium Events. Violators Will Be Ticketed and/or Towed Away at Their Own Expense." The fading, peeling, pitting and rusting are extreme. The script is outlined in black, faded away to white in numerous spots.

The large print words "No Parking During Stadium Events" was probably all red, most of which have faded to white. The background, which is now predominantly red, was likely white originally. The red hue owes to years of exposure to the harsh wintry elements. The lower sentence, "Violators Will Be Ticketed and/or Towed Away at Their Own Expense" appears more white today, but it was likely black in the original form. Someone disagreed with or did not understand this sign, as a question mark was spray-painted some years ago.

OPPOSITE County Stadium's "No Parking" sign is one of the last remnants from the ballpark located on General Mitchell Boulevard.

KD AUTO

Sometimes, signs leave behind a mystery waiting to be unraveled. Nevertheless, they have a story to tell and a legacy to cherish. As a "ghost-sign hunter," I can easily say that this has been one of the more puzzling signs I have encountered over the years. It is extremely frustrating to search endlessly, turning over stone after stone, and still come up empty-handed. Locals have shared a few anecdotes, but they typically sound like, "Oh, yes. I remember that place."

This lighted sign appears as though it has been nonfunctional for decades. Neglected with a broken acrylic outer shell, the sign sat above the main entrance door and was likely backlit with a faint yellow or white light when operational. "KD Auto" was interchangeably referred to as "KD" as well as "K and D." Located on South First Street in a Cream City brick building, KD Auto was an auto and truck body repair shop run by "Ken and Don." Beyond that little piece of information, this sign and the business it represents remain a mystery.

KD Truck & Auto is long gone, but the signs were still on the side of the building in 2017. Since then, the signs have been covered up.

KIPP'S SUPPER CLUB

Located at 5132 West Mill Road, a 2017 deconstruction of the Broadway Baby Dinner Theatre sign, which closed in 2010, revealed a surprise: a sign for Kipp's Supper Club. Owned by Herbert Kipp beginning in 1975, it was believed to be in operation until the early 1990s. The restaurant was decorated with dark paneling and had private meeting rooms or halls available for rent in addition to the main dining room.

This formerly lighted marquee sign had changeable lettering and must have been quite eye-catching decades ago. With medieval qualities influencing the design, it gives us pause to wonder if the interior had an "olde English" flair. Perhaps coats of armor decorated the walls and cast-iron chandeliers lit up the dim dining rooms?

The lettering reads as follows:

HNK [assumed to be the initials for Hebert Kipp]
RENTAL [with the letter "T" in reversed order and obstructed by the letter "A." Haphazardly slid out-of-place phone digits]

The black box with arrow affixed on the right sits directly underneath a spotlight. Looking closely, although it is incredibly faint, it looks like this may have at one time read "Seating." Maybe this was a signal that walk-in seating was available?

What exactly is a supper club? One thing is for certain: visiting a supper club is a "must" when in Wisconsin! A supper club is a family-owned restaurant that is open only for dinner, or the less formal "supper." The food is typically homemade, and likely the items have changed little since the establishment's inception, most of which started between 1940 and 1960. What makes supper clubs intriguing is that those still in operation boast an interior that remains virtually untouched, with original fixtures and furniture. The decor is often "stuck" in time from half a century prior, fully complemented by uniformed waitstaff and bartenders in styles reflecting that era. Other times, you will find the appeal of a Northwoods lodge-like setting, providing a more rustic feel. Despite the crisp white-clothed tables, these supper clubs are typically casual.

One of the unique features is that upon entering, diners are escorted directly to the bar, where a menu awaits and the libation of choice is promptly served. Without a doubt, the most commonly ordered is the

Kipp's Supper Club

JHK

FEDERAL

BAR OPEN

LA L
RENAL
41 4
212 5 13 2

unofficial state drink: the Brandy Old Fashioned. The bartender, not the waitstaff in this case, takes the food order. After a short time, the waitstaff escorts the guests to the table in the dining room, most often with a decadent relish tray waiting to be enjoyed. Typical surf-and-turf choices make up the menu, most of which are locally caught and farmed. If one chooses not to indulge in a dessert, a boozy ice-cream drink is a must-have alternative. Brandy Alexanders and, my personal choice, the Grasshopper, top the list as favorites in Milwaukee and across the state.

One of the first supper clubs I went to with my parents as a child was the Ishnala Supper Club, located in Wisconsin Dells on the picturesque Mirror Lake. I remember this impressive lodge set among mature pine and oak trees with dozens of floor-to-ceiling windows, each seat having a perfect view of the tranquil waters below. Not surprising, I found this whole process and the menu to be incredibly boring as this was not the typical place I thought of as "fun." Having not been a guest of Ishnala since sometime in the 1980s, I revisited it several years ago. Much to my surprise, nothing had changed. It was exactly as I had remembered it as a child. The only difference now was that I could appreciate the nostalgia, the quality food and, of course, the Grasshopper.

OPPOSITE A recent peeling of this sign revealed that it was for a restaurant called Kipp's Supper Club on Fifty-Second Street and Mill Road.

WINDUP LANES

This sign is fading as rapidly as the bowling industry itself in Milwaukee. This barely legible sign is still erected at 6416 West Greenfield Avenue in West Allis. Clearly visible, we still can read the name of the establishment as "Windup Lanes" in the bottom, rectangular light box. Flashing lights, no longer operational, decorate the entire perimeter of the sign. The print on the long vertical piece has completely worn off. It is very difficult to decipher what may have been there at one time. It is quite impressive, though, that the army green color of the neon sign matches the paint trim on the windows and shutters. I wonder which came first?

Irwin Leon was the proprietor in the early days of Windup Lanes. Not like the typical bowling centers we are accustomed to today, these wooden lanes were few and far between. I would guess that anywhere from six to ten lanes at most could be accommodated by a space this small. In operation long before automatic scoring was available, the lanes also probably utilized manual pin setting at one time.

Most evenings were probably bustling with league bowling. Bowling, historically referred to as a blue-collar sport, appealed to the "average Joe" as a way to enjoy competitive fun with friends while sharing pitchers of an ice-cold Milwaukee beer. My impression is that the ambiance overall was dark, with wood-paneled walls. The stench of cigarette smoke hung heavily in the air, embedded in the walls and carpeting. The classic bar was decorated with posters, snazzy beer signs and schedules for local sports teams. The familiar smashing and crashing of balls smacking down the pins was often drowned out by the hollers of frustration and shouts of joy and celebration.

Milwaukee was once the "bowling capital of the world" and home to the ABC (American Bowling Congress) until 2008, when the headquarters moved to Texas. Bowling and beer have long been synonymous with Milwaukee, spoofed in pop culture by the 1970s sitcom *Laverne and Shirley*, set in the city. Who can forget the hilarious episodes in which Laverne and Shirley, wearing matching bowling shirts, competed in league bowling with sidekicks Lenny and Squiggy?

In the 1960s, there were approximately 15,000 bowling centers across the United States. The popularity of bowling surged well into the 1980s, as evident by the locally hosted and produced television show *The Bowling Game*. Here, local teams would battle it out and compete for a monetary prize. The number of bowling centers has steadily been declining and plummeted to just over 4,650 in 2014.

Windup Lanes closed in the mid-1970s, a few decades before the nationwide plummet in popularity. The sign reminds us how much bowling was part of the fabric that once was Milwaukee.

OPPOSITE Windup Lanes dates to the 1960s on Sixty-Fourth Street and West Greenfield Avenue in West Allis. A couple of years ago, the sign was uncovered after Crawdaddy's restaurant moved to a new location.

SULLIVAN'S

We can still see neon tubing outlining all but a few letters for this gorgeous sign, located at 4714 South Packard Avenue in Cudahy.

Based on the work provided at Sullivan's, the store catered nearly exclusively to men. It was a one-stop shop for smoking supplies, a shoeshine and a hat blocking. Joe Salvatore and his wife, Mary, were fixtures in the community. They owned and operated the shop every day for nearly sixty years, opening their doors in 1931. They knew everyone who walked through the door by name. They knew their professions and the names of their children. It was a time when neighborhood and local stores flourished and thrived. Customer service and loyalty were central to how business was conducted.

As Joe and Mary were childless, Joe provided work and mentorship to dozens of teenage boys over the years. He allowed them to shine shoes and assist with basic tasks. Overall, he wanted to instill a strong work ethic and a sense of responsibility and accountability. Sullivan's was also said to have an active card room in the rear, which often included local politicians and community figures of the time.

When Joseph passed away in 1995, Mary continued to run the shop until 2010, retiring at the age of ninety-six

RIGHT Sullivan's Shine Parlor and Cigar Store in Cudahy closed many years ago, but the beautiful storefront remains intact.

GOLDMANN'S DEPARTMENT STORE

I am very persistent when it comes to things I am passionate about. My love of photography, while extending across a variety of subjects, has focused primarily on painted ads and road signs. When a sign is facing destruction, I am typically there documenting the event, taking photos with one hand while recording video with the other. The Goldmann's Department Store sign is one that, more than any other sign in this collection, held a special place in my heart. I relish the fond memories of my grandparents Leo and Florence Pinkert taking me to Goldmann's for lunch at the counter.

As noted in previous chapters, Mitchell Street was the heart of Milwaukee's South Side shopping. Polish and German immigrants shopped at Goldmann's for clothing and had a seat at the lunch counter to strike up a conversation and make new friends. You could always find what you wanted at Goldmann's. If you couldn't find something at other stores, you would most certainly find it there. Established in 1895, the department store would eventually struggle to compete with the larger, big-box retailers, and was forced to close its doors in 2007.

In August 2015, the original building underwent major renovations and the sign was removed. Dean C. Castelaz, Lynn Moritz and I discovered the sign in the parking lot behind the store. The series of events that would take place moving forward is quite riveting. Shortly after it was discovered, the sign was sold with my assistance to the National Save the Neon Sign Museum in Minot, North Dakota. The sign spent almost three years in Minot before returning back home to Milwaukee in March 2018, where it was stored in a temporary outdoor location until an appropriate showroom could be secured. I strongly felt that the sign should be displayed and enjoyed by the Milwaukee public and pursued every possible location and venue in the city. The restoration costs were estimated at nearly $20,000, which was a daunting amount of money to raise. Consequently, this steep investment turned away prospective buyers. Time was of the essence, as it was deeply concerning that the sign was outdoors, having to withstand the harsh Wisconsin winters. After multiple failed attempts to secure it a new home here, the sign left Milwaukee for the final time on October 7, 2019, and arrived at the American Sign Museum in Cincinnati, Ohio, the following day. Here, it will proudly represent Milwaukee and stand shoulder to shoulder with other vintage signs for future generations to enjoy.

ABOVE The Goldmann's Department Store sign is something near and dear to my heart. The store was open for 111 years, closing for good in 2007.

INDEX

ABOUT THE AUTHOR

A self-described "ghost-sign hunter," Adam Levin is a Milwaukee history buff and amateur photographer. He has intertwined his two favorite passions and channeled it into a successful following. As the administrator of the popular Facebook group "Old Milwaukee," he expanded this social media platform to share photos and tidbits from the past with thousands of Milwaukeeans. Through the group, the public has a convenient and accessible place to preserve memories through photographs and appreciate the rich history of the Cream City.

Possessing a fervorous fascination and deep curiosity of life and time that predated his own, it is no surprise that Adam favored history classes above all others while growing up. Upon recommendation from a teacher, while attending Nicolet High School on Milwaukee's North Shore, he enrolled in his first introduction to photography class in 1989. The teacher's intuition was right: Adam excelled, and he was hooked.

After graduating the following year from Nicolet High School, he subsequently enrolled in photography classes at the University of Minnesota and Milwaukee Area Technical School. In these, he explored the importance of color and intensity, lighting, composition, and additional fundamentals. Adam has an inherently keen eye for spotting the tiny subtleties that can be the difference between producing an ordinary photograph and a more creative and interesting one. A penchant toward seeking unique angles, patterns, shadows, and colors, he aims to create an overall unique composition with every photograph he takes.

After school, he found employment at K&S Photographics where he processed and developed commercial film. Despite the enjoyment he received from this line of work, he chose a different career path that resulted in putting his true passion temporarily on hold.

Nearly fifteen years later, in 2012, his passion was reignited. In fact, it became an obsession. Marrying his fascination with history and love for photography, he set out on a new path. While he initially focused his rebirthed hobby on historic architecture, he incidentally discovered a new love inscribed on those walls: ghost signs. In 2016, he briefly left Milwaukee, relocating to New Jersey for approximately two years. The proximity to New York City gave him the opportunity to explore the wondrous nooks and crannies of New York City, using every adventure as another opportunity to continue honing his photography skills.

When not wandering the city photographing building demolitions or newly revealed signs, one can often spot him perusing relics of the past in one of many local antique stores.